The Wind Off
the Island

THE MARINER'S LIBRARY

THE MARINER'S LIBRARY

THE WIND OFF THE ISLAND

ERNLE BRADFORD

GRAFTON BOOKS

A Division of the Collins Publishing Group

LONDON GLASGOW
TORONTO SYDNEY AUCKLAND

Grafton Books
A Division of the Collins Publishing Group
8 Grafton Street, London WIX 3LA

First published 1960
This Mariner's Library edition
published by Grafton Books 1988

British Library Cataloguing in Publication Data

Bradford, Ernle
  The wind off the island.
  1. Sicily – Description and travel –
  1946–1980
  I. Title
  914.5′804925   DG864.2

ISBN 0-246-13276-0

Printed and bound in Great Britain by
Mackays of Chatham Ltd, Chatham, Kent

O litus vita mihi dulcius, o mare! felix
cui licet ad terras ire subinde meas!
O formosa dies! hoc quondam rure solebam
Naiadas alterna sollicitare manu!
Hic fontis lacus est, illic sinus egerit algas:
Haec statio est tacitis fida cupidinibus.
Pervixi: neque enim fortuna malignior unquam
eripiet nobis quod prior hora dedit.

Petronius Arbiter

O shore dearer to me than life! O sea! How happy am I
with leave to come into these lands of mine. How beautiful
the day! Here once upon a time I used to swim, disturbing
Naiads with my every stroke! And here's the fountain's
heart, and there the seaweed waves. This is the haven of
my quiet desire. Yes, I have lived! Nor can an unkind fate
take from me ever gifts of that former hour.

SPRING

Huc ades, O Galatea; quis est nam ludus in undis?
Hic ver purpureum, varios hic flumina circum
fundit humus flores, hic candida populus antro
imminet et lentae texunt umbracula vites:
huc ades; insani feriant sine litora fluctus.

Virgil. Eclogue IX

Come here, my Galatea. Still playing in the sea? But here's
the brilliant spring, and by the stream the earth is bright
with flowers. Over my cave a silver poplar leans and the
vines cling to weave their shade. Come then, and let the
white surf thunder on the shore.

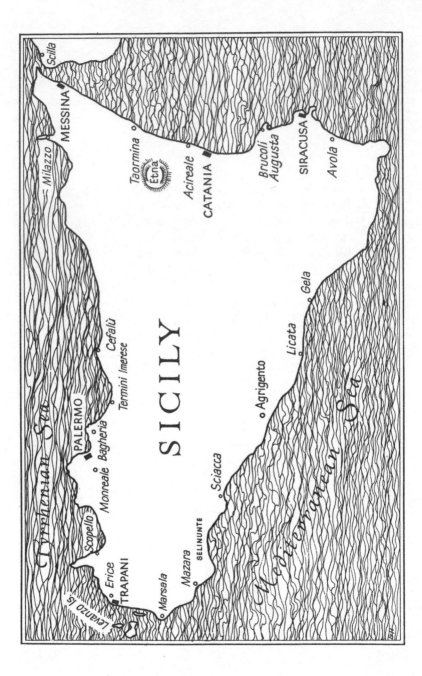

SICILY

Tyrrhenian Sea

Mediterranean Sea

Scilla

MESSINA

Milazzo

Taormina
Etna
Acireale
CATANIA

Brucoli
Augusta
SIRACUSA
Avola

Gela

Licata

Cefalù
Termini Imerese

Agrigento

PALERMO
Monreale Bagheria

Scopello

Sciacca

SELINUNTE

Erice
TRAPANI

Mazara

Marsala

Levanzo Is.

ONE

ALL night the sirocco has been blowing. The swell is running long and deep in the harbour, and the fishing boats are rolling. Their painted sides are stained where their old nails weep with rust. Their masts of pine describe wide arcs against the sky.

Sitting in the cockpit of *Mother Goose* I watch the day begin. The baroque houses of Trapani disclose their fruit and swags of flowers and fat-bottomed cherubs. It was dark when we reached the harbour last night, and this is my first sight of the old town.

A fisherman, his face misted in white stubble, rows past, making heavy weather of it in the sloppy harbour water. His back bends and stoops as he gets his shoulders into the work. He rows standing up, the way they all do here in Sicily.

'*Buon giorno, signore.* Evil weather!'

'Brutal. But I think the wind will die. The barometer rises.'

They never believe in my barometer. He spits over the gunwale of his boat and shakes his head.

'More wind to come, signore.'

I watch him plugging away up the harbour. The spray lifts and flickers before the blunt bows. He is wearing only a shirt and a pair of patched trousers. The wind moulds them to his wet body and shakes his grey hair.

The kettle on the primus stove begins to sigh, then its melancholy note tells me the water is boiling. Janet is still asleep. She had the middle watch—from twelve to four. It is six o'clock on the morning of April the fourteenth, and the barometer I note in the log has risen from 1017 to 1020 millibars. I light a cigarette and make myself a pot of tea. The first cup of the day and the first cigarette taste good in the clean, sea-smelling air. The sirocco is always a warm wind and, although it blows hard, there is little bite in it.

It was just beginning to pipe up when we made harbour last night. We were on our way to Palermo, but the falling barometer and the splayed fingers of cirrus that trailed across the sky warned us to take shelter. We came in on the bearing of the lighthouse, and all night we have lain under its shuttling fan. The moon was up, nearly full, when we came through the breakwater. That had made it easy to find the end of the long mole, noisy with the suck and swallow of the sea. The mole was studded with ugly teeth, where concrete blocks had fallen in during the winter.

As we altered course for Trapani I had remembered the old rhyme:

> The hollow winds begin to blow;
> The clouds look black, and the glass is low.
> Last night the sun went pale to bed;
> The moon in haloes hid her head.
> Look out, my lads! A wicked gale
> With heavy rain will soon assail.

The clouds had been banking up dark along the horizon and the sun had been the colour of straw as it set to the west of Sicily. The hollow winds had been murmuring in the rigging and the moon had been circled by three haloes, pale opal against the straining clouds.

I poured the remains of the hot water into a bowl, propped a mirror against the coil of the mainsheet, and began to lather my face. I had a day and a half's beard and a salt-rimed skin. It was good to feel the skin coming up new and fresh, almost as if I were shaving away the years. When I had finished I took a look over the side. Trapani was quite a big place and I didn't like bathing in the big Sicilian harbours, knowing that all the drainage, not only from the ships but from the whole town, poured into them. Still, the sirocco had swept the harbour clean, and there was a current of clear water setting past the boat. It was driven in by the swell through the jaws of the breakwater.

I slung the rope ladder over the side—in case the swell made getting back aboard difficult—and dropped over. Although it was early spring the water was quite warm, beaded with bubbles of spray. I swam a little way out from the boat, then turned and paddled on my back, looking at *Mother Goose* as she slopped and rolled in the early light.

She was a ten-ton Dutch Boeier, built of iron and painted dark blue. Designed as a racing Boeier, she had a higher mast than most of her kind, and the broad oak fans of her leeboards were a perfect aerofoil shape. You

14

could not call her graceful, she was too chubby for that. She was comely though. Her red-tanned sails contrasted with the white of her teak decks and the royal blue of her sides to make her an ornament in any harbour. As she rolled I watched the long pennant of her wimpel—the Dutchman's weather-vane—circle and stagger, then blow out straight again in the south-east wind. She heaved her russet anti-fouling paint clear of the water, then sank down until the exhaust-pipe was below the surface. As she rose once more, the empty pipe spat out the water in a derisive gurgle. (The sound of it had been one of the last things I had heard as I dropped off to sleep at midnight.) *Mother Goose* was thirty feet long. She had been our home now for over a year—ever since we had crossed the bar at Chichester and headed south for the sun and the dolphin sea.

The light was already beginning to lift along the roof-tops of Trapani. The clouds were thinning, and the buildings were no longer an unresolved mass but a hundred and one details, sharpening in the lemony glow. As I swam slowly back, a fishing boat came chugging past, her heavy diesel knocking on the air and her exhaust blowing smoke-rings above the deckhouse. Seven or eight men lined the side. They called to me; one waved; another made the gesture of pulling off his jersey as if to join me.

'*Pazzo!*' they would be saying to each other. 'Crazy like a hare!'

Not many of the fishermen could swim, although they would some-times loll in the shallow waters on the blinding summer days when the lion-sun had made the land too hot to touch. I had seen many *ex-votos* in Sicilian churches which showed sailors being washed ashore on planks, or drifting to safety leashed to broken spars. The credit was always given to the Virgin, the Star of the Sea—never to the victim's ability to swim. In Sicily the offices of Venus, ancient goddess of sailors, have mostly been taken over by the Virgin.

I dried myself on deck, with one of the old yellowing towels, harsh-tongued with salt and sand, that we kept for bathing. Then I went round the boat for the morning inspection. There was always something to be done; there always is in a boat, but especially if you live in one. The end of one of the halliards needed whipping. It was time we changed the main-sheet end for end. The wire seizing had come off the eye of the shackle to the topping-lift. I felt the mainsail with the flat of my hand—damp. It was damp not from any spray or rain, but from the heavy dew that the sirocco always brings. After breakfast we would hoist it and let it dry off.

I was washing down the foredeck, wrinkling my toes in the salt water and brooming some fine, blown sand from behind the capstan, when Janet put her head out. She was still drugged with sleep.

'Sorry for the noise,' I said.

'That's okay. What's the time?'

'Getting on for eight.'

'I might as well wash and wake up then.'

We had breakfast sitting out in the cockpit. In that warm land one lives more on the upper deck than below. That's one reason why we did not tire of the confined space of a small boat. We lived outside, with the spring world as our drawing-room. Every day, or almost every day, we changed the decoration of our home—all we had to do was get up the anchor and move somewhere else.

The scent of coffee was on the air. We had large plates of eggs, bacon, slices of aubergine, and the crusty brown bread we had bought two days before in Sciacca.

'Sleep well?'

'Like a log,' she said.

'This is the life.'

We were sitting over cigarettes and a last cup of coffee when the boat came out to us from the Capitaneria del Porto. Italians love forms and documentation, and I carried the same papers as if I had been a trading schooner or a large merchant ship. Every time that we left one port for another I had to declare my destination. It was futile, of course, for often the wind and weather made us put into some harbour other than the one we had intended. Quite apart from that, if we liked the look of a place we ambled out of our way and visited it. The authorities never seemed to mind the fact that I was always turning up in the wrong port, but they still insisted—while admitting the whole thing was farce—that I must comply with regulations. Documents, forms, restrictions, are the curse of our modern world; but here, in Sicily, taken always with a grain of salt, with a good-natured shrug of the shoulders.

'*Buon giorno, Capitano!*'

White teeth flash in a lean olive face, and his hands are immaculate. They contrast harshly with our own broken finger-nails and calloused palms. The lieutenant's nails are scrupulously kept. The little finger of the left hand is about two inches long: the caste mark which shows he is not a member of the labouring classes. He expresses the usual astonishment that there are only two of us, refuses to believe that a woman can be anything other than a passenger—and accepts a whisky (early though it is) 'just to try the taste'. I keep a little whisky on board specially for port authorities and Customs officers. Whisky is 'very snob', and to have tasted it gives them a pleasant cachet among their friends.

'You come from Malta?'

'Yes, we have passed the winter there.'

'But you prefer Sicily?'

'Naturally,' I said.

'The Maltese are not Italians, nor English. I have been there, I know. They are Moors. An unsympathetic people.'

Before he leaves, he advises us to move further down the harbour. At the far end we will find a quiet corner where some fishing boats are being repaired. We can lie alongside one of them, which will mean that we can step straight ashore without having to put the dinghy in the water. We are duly grateful to him.

The wind is still blowing hard as we get up the anchor and motor to our new berth. The air is soft, though, and I am sure that the sirocco will die before the day is out. Broken sunlight is running along the roof-tops of Trapani, and the cloud base is lifting.

We make fast against the rough wooden sides of a fifty-ton fishing boat. There is nobody aboard her, but a watchman crawls out from a shack on the foreshore and gives us a hand with our lines. He has a cigarette and a cup of coffee with us, swears that the wind will last another two days, and that the spring is late in coming this year. For some cigarettes, a few lire, and a tin of coffee he will be most pleased to look after our boat while we are in Trapani. I learned my lesson when I was in Sicily last year: always engage a local man, even if the duties are nominal, to keep an eye on things. The word soon gets round that you have paid for your security. The mafia only troubles the locals—and the rich. We are small fry, and not worth bothering about. But even small birds of passage, if they are wise, will make some contribution.

'You go ashore now, you and your lady? Tell me what you want and I will tell you where to buy.'

We need little but eggs and bread, some fresh vegetables, and some wine. He tells us where the market lies, and where there is a good wine-shop. It is run by his cousin; we need only say that Mario Lo Bianco sent us. Lo Bianco, 'The White One': I wonder how his family came by the name—some joke, maybe, many centuries ago, for he is one of the Sicilians whose dark skin and hawklike features tell of a North African ancestry.

Janet takes the string bag, I the empty demijohn, and we step ashore for the first time in three days. Just beyond the fishing boat a stream wanders sluggishly into the harbour. The grass along its banks is enamel green. Small stagnant shallows alternate with patches of grass, clover, and

17

wild sea fern. We have to wander some way down the bank looking for a crossing-place, and then we are over into a field where a pathway leads to the town.

'Look!' Janet takes my arm.

The whole field is brilliant with wild flowers. As the wind shakes the tangled grass, they nod and curtsey and recover—pink snapdragons and small blue irises. There are gladioli and bee orchids. By the ruined wall of a cottage we come upon wild cyclamen. The wind is letting up, the clouds are lifting, and the spring has come over Sicily. When we left Malta the small square fields, bounded with their stone walls, had been bright with clover, but there was nothing like this milky-way of wild flowers.

An old man carrying an oar on his shoulder passes us, heading inland. A sailor looking for a place in which to retire? The flowers remind me that it was here in Trapani that Anchises, the father of Aeneas, died. As a young man he had been the lover of Venus, who bore him one son—the future founder of Rome. Carried from the flaming ruins of Troy on his son's shoulders, the old man had survived to see Sicily, and to die here. Perhaps it was on a day like this he died, with the flowers to remind him of his own springtime and of his youthful beauty which had made the Queen of Love take him to her bed. A dangerous thing getting involved with a goddess, even mortal women are difficult enough.

'I bet you forgot to ask the watchman where we could find a glazier and get the skylight fixed.'

'Damn. Yes, I'm sorry. So I did,' I said.

'Drepanon', the Greeks called Trapani—'a sickle'. It lies on a low spit of land which curves from north-east to south-west. Even the names have the continuity of centuries in this island. One never feels cut off from the past, isolated in the present, as one does in more modern countries. Here in Sicily the dead voices and the rhythms of ancient life and the youth of the world are always just over your shoulder. Sometimes, swimming in a quiet bay, or watching the dawn come up over the sea, you cannot remember in what century you live. You are only aware of yourself as a man, born for a brief confusion of pleasure and pain, and then to go back into the dark again—like those small blue irises we saw, which bloom one morning and are dead by sunset.

Shopping is pleasant. We always take an hour or more over it, even when we buy no more than three or four things. Each stall, each small dark doorway, catches the eye with its wooden trays and shelves—dappled mullet, oranges and mandarins, pasta as varied as shells on the seashore, plaited loaves and rolls sprinkled with caraway seeds, and rich slabs of *ricotta*, the sugar-sweetened local cheese. This morning, as usual, we are in no hurry. We idle among the vegetable stalls and come away with anis-smelling roots of fennel, two kilos of the small plum tomatoes, fresh basil, and oranges. The oranges still have the life of the tree inside them. When I press the skin of one of them, a faint blue mist spurts into the air. It scents my hand with its clean, sunny bitterness.

By winding alleys that break out every now and then into old squares, we make our way down to the long promenade that faces the sea. We pass many houses with that withdrawn quality which the Spaniards bring to their architecture. They look inwards, and turn blank walls interspersed with narrow, grille windows on to the street. Through wrought-iron gates we see courtyards, trees, few flowers as yet, but in one or two of them there is the plash of water.

The long promenade, where in the evening everyone of distinction will make their *passegiata*—idly to and fro, eyeing each other, inventing scandals, dreaming up liaisons, architecting future marriages—is deserted today. Wind booms over the walls. A little spray flickers and rises across the pavement and the street.

'The horizon's better,' said Janet. 'Look, you can see some of the islands.'

To the south-west we can see the outline of Formica, and beyond it— like a grey cloud—something else. Levanzo perhaps?

'Let's take a look at the islands when the weather lets up.'

So we shall go next to the Aegadian islands. Little known to visitors, off all the shipping routes, of little importance in history—except once only when, at about this time of the year, the Roman Fleet defeated the Carthaginians somewhere in these narrow waters. The battle took place between where we stand and the neighbouring islands. It was not blowing a sirocco then. The galleys were under oars when the Romans tried out their new tactics of grappling irons and close-in fighting. The sea ran red that day, as it still does when the great tunny are being gaffed in the nets off Favignana.

In the afternoon, while Janet worked on cleaning and repainting the galley, I cut out the broken skylight frame from the putty.

'Sure, Captain,' said Mario, 'there is a glazier in the town. But look, I'll tell you what we do. Now—if *you* go in and order a new glass, they will know you are a foreigner.' He plucked at his ear, not wishing to offend. 'True, you speak Italian, but not Sicilian. Eh—and then you have fair hair! They think you're a German perhaps. Anyway, they charge you too much money. You give me the glass. I'll take it in this evening. I will tell them it comes from the ship I am looking after—and so we shall pay the right price. I think I can get a new one for five hundred lire.'

'I asked at a ship chandler's this morning,' I said. 'I told them the size. They said it would cost about two thousand.'

'Surely. I know them. They take one thousand five hundred for themselves, and pay the glazier five. You leave things to me, Captain.'

The day passed swiftly as we worked about the boat. There was no swell at this end of the harbour and we lay easily against our neighbour.

In the evening the clouds had gone. A wind-washed sky opened up overhead. It was blue all the way to the south of us, right down to Africa. As the sun went down, the mountain of San Giuliano rose out of the lowlands behind Trapani and began to glow like amber. There were still clouds around its head, but all the tree-grown sides and the bare scarp to the south were catching the light.

'We'll go there tomorrow, shall we?' Janet pointed.

'Yes, we could leave Mario in charge. There's a bus up in the morning, and back again at night.'

Mario came over and took the pane of glass.

'I will be back in an hour or two, if you and your lady wish to go into the town.'

'Would it be all right to go before you're back?' I asked.

'Yes. Lock the boat. But no one will touch her.'

We had pasta followed by roast chicken—a well-muscled Olympic runner—in a small tavern. The wine was good, a wine from Alcamo, a village in the hills behind Trapani. It was a soft greenish-yellow, and quite dry. Afterwards we went over to a café where some of the local youths dreamed over a juke-box. We had black coffee and a marsala. The marsala was too sweet for my taste. It had compensations though, a rich colour like autumn, and a bouquet that contained all the dark roundness of the grape.

'Here's to our Sicilian year!' Janet raised her glass.

The sky was quite clear as we walked back to the boat. The air was still damp but it was warm, raising from the earth the scent of new grass and of all the scattered flowers. Mario was sitting in the entrance to his hut, a can of coffee on a brazier in front of him.

'The beautiful weather comes now,' he said. 'Tomorrow will be fine for you to go to Erice.'

'Good night,' I said.

'Good night, Captain, good night to you and the lady. That, and a healthful sleep.'

TWO

ALL the way from the flat lands of the coast the bus mounts skywards. We look back and see the white shine of the salt pans between Marsala and Trapani, and the grey-blue plain of the sea, heaving slightly after the sirocco. The bus shudders to a halt in a small village. The front wheels are close to the edge of a sheer drop and a crackling argument breaks out, the driver turning to shout at a passenger in the seat behind him.

'What goes on?' I said.

'I think he's stopping to put someone down—or pick someone up. The fat man doesn't like the look of the cliff edge.'

We sat there for five minutes.

I could hardly blame those in front for asking the driver to back a little. The land fell clean away to the fertile plain below—no need to make it more fertile, I thought.

'English sang-froid—stiff upper lip,' said Janet.

'I wish I'd brought some brandy.'

A carabiniere joined the bus and we edged away from the cliff. Just before we got under way the driver stood up and pointed at the fat man. With one hand he made the gesture of shaking out the seat of his pants.

'*Paura!*' he laughed.

'*Paura!*' I said. 'I don't blame him for being afraid.'

Two and a half thousand feet up we shudder to a halt. Here is Erice, old and grey, and deep in the clouds. The mists here are famous. Almost the first thing the curator of the museum asked me was whether our London fogs could compare.

'They don't,' I said. 'Because in London they're full of factory smoke, diesel and petrol fumes, and sulphur. These can only give you rheumatism.'

'Progress is not always progress,' he said. 'Yes, these are only clouds.

Once they hid the shrine of Venus, and all her handmaids, and all the sacred doves.'

As we stood talking at the doorway of the museum the clouds went up high over our heads, with a sweep and a billow like the lifting of a muslin dress. The sun came through, and from the ramparts of the castle we could see all the western plains of Sicily, as far as Castellammare and right south to Marsala and the coast. There were more clouds drifting across from Africa, a scattered argosy of cumulus that beached themselves and broke up on the foothills below us. Here, where we stood, was once the great temple of Venus Erycina.

Janet took a breath. 'This is air!'

The scarred sides of the mountain were dense with pine. The dampness and the new warmth from the sun combined to fill the air with their tingling needle scent, and cool privet from the nearby gardens blended with the pine. If one could wake every morning with that air in one's lungs one might live for a hundred years. I wondered how long the handmaidens of Venus lived. Were they pensioned off after a time? Even under the Roman occupation this shrine still had its own inviolable territory, and paid no tribute to the conquerors. Even Verres, archetype of all military looters, who plundered everywhere else in Sicily, left the temple of Venus Erycina alone.

Hand in hand two Nordic lesbians wandered through the quiet gardens and embraced under a cypress.

'Exiles from Taormina?'

The museum curator looked at them. '*L'amore*,' he said, without a smile and with no irony.

There is a feeling of love in the air of Erice, yet, strangely enough, it is not the sensual love one associates with the goddess. Here it is tender, wistful, and un-Sicilian. Somehow the clouds, when they drive through the streets in long grey streamers, bring all the northern nostalgia with them. Perhaps that was why the Normans who lived and built here felt at home in Erice.

'In winter,' said the curator, 'there are always clouds. In winter it always rains.'

When the gutters gushed from the houses and from the beaked spouts of the cathedral the Normans must have felt that this was another *pot de chambre*, like Rouen. The difference was that here the rain would slip swiftly away down the screes and crags, and the sun would come through again.

Looking to the west, from the edge of the Roman walls, we could see the far-off huddle of Trapani. Beyond it, as the light cleared, the Aegadian islands were lifting their pale heads out of the sea.

'That's where we go next,' I said. 'Favignana. Levanzo. Marettimo.'

Snails' tracks trailed across the water, quite visible from this height: the wakes of fishing boats and small coasters. Out by Formica a wing flickered—one of the schooners was hoisting a steadying sail to hold her against the southerly swell.

In the cathedral the ceiling was a golden lacework. Women in black, with the faces of wrinkled walnuts, were knotting their brown-veined hands and kneeling beside their chosen altars. A man with the sad face of a spaniel stared into space, a cloth cap on his knees. His boots were heavy with yellow earth and dust. He must have walked here from some village far down in the valley.

The clouds were streaming through the streets again when we came out. The ancient walls were sinister, and driving veils of nimbus were streaking through the empty arches and blind windows. The edge of a raincloud was visible where it divided. On our side we were dry, but over there—only a few yards away—heavy drops were starring the stone flags. In the main piazza we found a small restaurant with scrubbed tables, flowers in hanging baskets on the walls, a local family eating pasta and beans, a black dog—and no one else. Lunch cost less than ten shillings— two camparis, a litre of good wine, two pastas, steak and salad, peaches, coffee, and bread.

'Remember Malta?' said Janet. 'They'll be eating roast beef and boiled potatoes now.'

'At ten bob a head sitting under a portrait of K.G. Five, in Rex's bar off Kingsway.'

In the cool of the evening the bus took us back to Trapani. Erice veiled itself and drew the night clouds over its fortress walls. A perfect place to defend! It was clear why this mountain had been a garrison town, ever since the Elymi settled here, long before the first Greek traders came cutting round Cape San Vito to disturb the sleepy sea.

Mario greeted us with the news that the chief of police had been round.

The old man grinned. 'Not to put you in prison, signore. The "capo" speaks good English and he wishes to practise it. I told him you had gone to Erice and would be back by the last bus. He will call again. He is a very gentle, very *simpatico*, man.'

We changed out of our shore-going clothes, I into overalls, Janet into old blue jeans. A woman wearing trousers ashore in Sicily would be an object of derision, and the target for all the wolves in town. The Sicilian knows that all foreign women are immoral in any case. He knows that they are only waiting for his bright smile and muscled arms to support him in the style to which he would like to be accustomed. He has good reason for his cynicism. He has heard about Capri; he has a cousin in Taormina who has given up fishing; and his uncle in Palermo married an American last year. What was it the young fisherman in Syracuse said to me as he showed me a platinum cigarette-case? Ah, yes—'Now, I can buy a new mainsail for the boat, and have a mass said for my mother.'

While Janet polished the saloon I dropped down into *Mother Goose*'s small engine-room and started the motor. We had a two-cylinder diesel engine that gave us about five knots. (We would need it in the windless days of summer.) It also charged the batteries for the twelve-volt lighting circuit. The engine started with a bang, and then settled down to its steady, slow-running chug. I nipped on deck and stared over the side to see that the cooling system was working. A drift of blue smoke rose from the exhaust-pipe, then a trickle of water started, then a steady stream. Now it made its familiar happy sound, a liquid purr like a big cat. Half an hour would be enough to top up the batteries.

'A good motor,' Mario said, looking down from the deck of the fishing boat. 'Diesel? How much do you pay for the fuel?'

I told him, and he raised his hands to the sky, with the palms upwards.

'You pay the same as lorries and motor-cars!'

'I'm only a visitor. I can't get it at fishing-boat rates.'

He winked. 'I'll fix it before you leave. You need twenty gallons? I'll see the owner of this boat. You pay him the same as he pays and we'll siphon it off from his tanks into yours. We'll do it tonight.'

The sun was going down behind the tumble of buildings on the far side of the harbour. A castle of cumulus caught fire behind the cathedral. Mario pointed and gestured around the sky.

'Beautiful weather coming.'

The saloon smelled of wax polish, and the mahogany panelling gleamed. Glasses were out on the table, small bowls of olives, black and green, and there were anchovies and cashew nuts. I got whisky from the locker for our guest, and a tin of English cigarettes.

For a small boat, *Mother Goose* had a lot of space, but standing head-room was the one thing she lacked—except just under the skylight. I should have hated to live in her month after month in England. But under an indulgent sky life is very different.

On the left, just as you came down the steps from the cockpit, there was a small galley with a stainless-steel sink and draining-board; a two-burner primus stove with an oven beneath; and two hand pumps, one for fresh and one for salt water. A forty-gallon tank of fresh water lay under the cockpit. There was a large locker below the sink where we kept all the kitchen gear, and a scuttle, opening out on to the upper deck, lifted the galley heat and smells away from the saloon. We used pressure cookers a great deal, they saved paraffin and made it easy to do a three-course meal. We had a second oven—a portable one, which fitted over the paraffin burners. Cakes, pastry, pies, and even bread had come out of it. Who wants to live in a boat if he is to be condemned to fried food all the time?

The chief of police was ushered aboard by Mario. He was in his fifties, ceremonious, with beautiful manners, and speaking good English. After the usual civilities, the handshakings, the compliments, the admiration of a woman's bravery for travelling in so small a boat, we relaxed round the saloon table. (Later we would do a tour of the boat, examine its wireless, the chart stowage, the galley, the heads even, and we would admire the view over our bows, where the peak of Erice was catching the light.)

'When I was young,' he said, 'I wanted to be a writer—in English, you understand, like Joseph Conrad.'

'Why not Italian?' I asked.

'The public is too small. Too few can read anyway and for the novel one must have big sales. Besides, the language is too sweet, too plastic. There is not enough spine. Have you read d'Annunzio?'

'A few pages. He is too like Strega and hair oil for my taste.'

'In Italian,' he said, touching his moustache with a white forefinger, 'it is difficult not to write like d'Annunzio. The temptation is always there —to be carried away by the rhetoric of our language. Sicilian would be better—Verga was a great writer—it is more masculine. But then, who can write for an audience of a few thousand?'

Of course he had never been able to go to England and make himself a Conrad. He came from an old family, long resident in Trapani, and proud to claim descent from the Aragonese. So he had gone into the public service. Then there had been the war. Now he was back again in his home town, and here he would stay.

Mario rapped on the hatch and diffidently put his head down. I went out and he whispered in my ear.

'The owner says it's all right about the diesel. We'll take it tonight and you pay him the same as he pays. He'll come back about ten o'clock.'

'That old fisherman,' said the chief of police, 'he is a good man. Your boat will be safe with him, if you come back here and wish again to go away for a day or more. Some are not so good. Of course we have many problems here in Sicily. The Church, illiteracy, and then of course there is the old movement.'

I never asked about the mafia. If they wanted to talk about it they would. It would not be impossible even for the chief of police to be involved in the 'old movement'. Many politicians and business men were. He said no more on the subject, but, just before he left, he gave me some good advice.

'If you are ever in a small fishing port, or somewhere where the people seem difficult, ask of a fisherman or in a *taverna* for the "capo"—I do not mean the chief of police. It may be that the "capo" will come and have a word with you, or it may be that the man you are talking to will ask you why you want to see him. All you say then is, that you want a good man to look after your boat. Either way you will get a reliable man—it will only cost a few lire—and you will never have any trouble.'

Out of our small library I found a few paperbacks that we did not want—*Fiesta*, *The Thirty-Nine Steps*, a Wodehouse, a Simenon, and *Pride and Prejudice*. He was delighted with the strange mixture. I like most of all to think of him sitting at home reading them on some sultry evening, when the old walls of Trapani are giving back the daytime heat with that sudden rise in temperature which follows the sunset breeze. I like to think of him, as the wind draws off the Mediterranean and stirs the dark alleys, slipping into the muslin tea-time world of Jane Austen. We would see him again when we came back to Trapani, and perhaps by then there would be more books that we could pass his way. It was difficult to get English books here in Sicily. When we got back to Malta I would send him some. He eyed the long rows of the *Encyclopaedia Britannica*, stacked in a bookcase in the engine-room, and touched their backs with greedy fingers.

'Is it safe to have those fine volumes in a small boat? I mean— supposing you were shipwrecked. What a loss!'

'It's one of the last things we would worry about.'

'Yes, yes, I suppose so. Still . . .'

At any rate, I knew now that—if we ever did have a misfortune on the wild coasts of Sicily—there was one man of authority who would be eager to arrange for our salvage.

After he had gone we had a simple *pasta al forno*, one good way of getting rid of spaghetti left over from an earlier meal. In the bottom of a greased and garlic-rubbed casserole we put first a layer of cooked spaghetti, then one of onions, another of spaghetti, a layer of tomatoes, and so on.

We alternated them with cooked meat and topped the dish with basil and parmesan. After a day of sun and clear air one ate well. Dance music from Rome mingled with the slop of the sea. The barometer was steady and the wind had veered to the north-east. Tomorrow we would have a light sailing breeze to carry us to the islands.

'*Signore! Capitano!*'

Mario again. With him was a squat, broad-shouldered man in a dark-blue suit, the fishing-boat owner. After handshakes and expressions of goodwill we set about transferring the fuel from his boat to mine. An hour later we could all relax in the cockpit and drink a little coffee. I handed round some American cigarettes (our English ones were too anaemic for most Italian palates). There was a bright moon and the sky was clear. The stretch of water between us and the town had a mottled burnish like hand-beaten silver.

After they had gone, the saloon suffered the nightly transformation, from living-room to bedroom. The back panels of the settees lifted up and were secured against the ship's side. The bunks slid out and the bedding, sheets, and sleeping-bags were unrolled.

'Good night. Sleep sound.'

Janet was one of the lucky ones who could turn in and be asleep within seconds. I suffer from 'book disease'. However tired I am, I can never sleep until I have read a few lines, or a few pages. That started during the war. I can remember coming off watch, tired out, and still having to look at some book, magazine, or old newspaper, before the hum of the destroyer's life faded away from me. I can remember one book that always sent me to sleep. God knows where I found it—Alexandria perhaps? It was published by the Society for Psychical Research, and called *Death, its Causes and Phenomena*. It had some depressing pictures, and I remember how my friend Martin reacted when he first saw it. A midshipman then, joining his first destroyer fresh from Dartmouth, he was a little taken aback.

'Good God! Is it that bad? You have to be prepared for everything?'

He happily talks of it years later, and still tells the story: 'Of course you got some odd types in the Navy during the war. . . .' I had lost that book years ago. On this night I had the *Admiralty Pilot for the Mediterranean*, Volume 1. It was good clear prose, with all the information well sifted, and quite often veins of poetry cropped out through its granite fact. I would look up the places we were going to visit: 'Levanzo. This rugged island had about 250 inhabitants in 1950. . . . Cala Dogana lies close westward of Cala Fredda, and in it is a beach. At the head of the cove is a village, where there is a landing-place. The bottom is sand and good holding ground.' That sounded a fine place to drop anchor for a few days. I had some work to do, and it was high time the typewriter rattled again in the saloon. The past few weeks had been too busy for anything other than the sea world. But I was not getting paid for being an amateur sailor, and if we were to keep eating I had to send something back to London.

There was a little wind during the night, and I got up once to check that our lines were not chafing and that our fenders held us comfortably away from the fishing-boat's rough side. Mario's brazier was still glowing, but the old man was asleep. There were no high cirrus clouds with the wind, no clouds at all, and I guessed it was only a land breeze drawing out to sea. Off the west coast of Italy they call it the 'Tramontana', the 'Cross-the-mountains' wind. It happens there almost every night, for the land cools quicker than the sea, and the air drops off the mountains in sudden gusts. It makes a scurry like footsteps over the dark waters, and you need to slack the mainsheet quickly before it hits you. There was no violence in this wind, though, and our lines held firm. It came from Erice and the north. I could turn in again and sleep peacefully till daybreak.

THREE

T HE boat was going well, with a bone between her teeth and a quick chuckle under her stern. The decks were just beginning to steam and there was a clean smell of wood and cordage.

A lone coaster sliced out of the morning sea, bound south. She was about five miles away—an old Liberty boat deep-loaded. There were still plenty of them plodding around the Mediterranean. Greek- or Italian-owned, she would have paid her way many years ago by now. Although she had the wind astern, her funnel smoke drifted aft. She could hardly be making more than ten knots, so the breeze must be even less.

'We'll be motoring within the hour,' said Janet. She was busy with metal polish and soft rags, shining up the brightwork. We still had old-fashioned brass fittings; they made another chore, but it was worth it for their friendly shine, unlike the coldness of our chromium age. The mainsail gave a flap as we lifted over the southern swell. Yes, the wind was dying.

Janet went below. 'I'll bring Captain Kidd up for an airing.'

Captain Kidd—I had almost forgotten him. He had been very quiet these last few days. Perhaps the soaking he got coming from Malta (when a sea broke down the open skylight) had made him off colour. Not ill, I hoped. But no, here he was preening himself in the morning sun, and repeating over and over again in a cracked voice: 'Pieces of eight! Pieces of eight!' A cock budgerigar of vivid green, the Captain had been with us all the way from England. A well-travelled bird by now, he had crossed the Channel, seen the Seine on misty mornings in spring, and heard the rush of the Seine-bore as it came up the river past Quilleboeuf—first a noise like wind far off in the pine trees, then an express train, and then the high wave on which *Mother Goose* had soared, lifted, and staggered. The Captain had woken on sunny mornings in Paris and had once been to a night-club where an existentialist child with green eye-shadow had worn him on her shoulder like a brooch. He knew the long stretches of the French canals, and the way the sunlight strikes down on you when you come out from the Pouilly tunnel, and see ahead the Canal de Bourgogne dropping away in a shining staircase, all the way to the valley of the Saône. Nearly lost in the basin at Dijon, he had heard the Rhône in spate, grown randy on the summer Riviera, and wandered the western coast of Italy. His vocabulary was limited: 'Pieces of eight! Captain Kidd! Have a drink!' and '*Merde!*' Like many another traveller, he had found that four or five phrases were enough to take him around.

Now the mainsail hung empty as a sailor's pockets, the sigh of moving water died away, and the boat began to roll and lurch over the deep-breathing swell. Together we dropped the main, then—while I started the engine—Janet lowered the jib. The decks were getting hot under our bare feet. Looking over the side into the water I could see a perfect cat's eye where some freak of light between sun and sea made that star effect one finds in a domed sapphire. I went back to the tiller.

'We're about halfway.' Janet pointed to the shining sides of Formica on our port beam. Levanzo lay only seven miles from Trapani: we would be there within the hour.

Two fishing boats, their lateen sails furled, their crew sweating at the rough-handled oars, crept out to us across the water. The rubbing strake of one was bright blue, the other chrome yellow. They had painted eyes on their bows (to see their way) and—though crudely built—they were well kept. In summer the men go out in those open boats all the way to the Kerkenah banks off Africa. They take dried fish, figs, and raisins with them, and a demijohn or two of water. Sometimes they are away for weeks, landing and selling their catch wherever they can. They are fine seamen, and their lives have a true dignity. All of them would like to emigrate to America, wear city suits, gold wristwatches, and snap-brim hats.

The leading boat was quite close to us now. Her helmsman waved and shouted something, as Janet eased the throttle and slipped the gear into neutral.

'Foreigners . . . a man and a woman.' The coxswain cracked his leathery face into a smile.

'Good day, Captain. You want fish?'

'What have you?'

I could see the baskets piled round their feet in the boat's bilges. They had mullet, dendici, gar-fish, dabs, and octopus.

'And squid,' said a lean youth in the bow. Relaxed and easy, he was leaning to the boat's lift and sway, his right arm twisted around the tired old forestay. Unlike the others, he had taken off his shirt and was wearing only a faded pair of khaki trousers. He was well muscled, graceful, and his skin was a light bronze.

'And squid, of course,' said the coxswain. 'And then . . .' He kicked aside an old sack at his feet: sea-coloured, rustling and snapping with dry clicks against the boat's wooden sole, the well-fleshed Mediterranean lobsters that they get off this coast.

We took two of them for five hundred lire and threw in a tin of coffee for a saucepan full to the brim with mullet. The second boat swung up close to us, her coxswain pointing to our leeboards. As always, Janet had to explain that they were not stabilizers to counteract sea-sickness, but a type of drop keel. That too was difficult to explain to fishermen, few of whom had seen even an ordinary centre-board. Their own boats were shallow draught and keel-less, and on the wind, to prevent making leeway, one of the crew stood up and rowed. I noticed there was no hostility between the two boats. Their owners were brothers and the crews were related. Whatever one of them took would be equally shared with the others.

'*Dove andate?*' asked the graceful youth.

'Levanzo. Is it a good anchorage?'

'Go well in, close by the village at the head of Cala Dogana,' he said. 'There is two metres right up to the houses. You are safe there from almost any wind.'

As we got under way, the two boats drew closer together. Now they would share out the money and decide where to sell the coffee when they got back to Formica. We had paid a fair price, but not too much, and they had made an unexpected sale. It was pleasant to do business on that basis, where everyone felt good about it afterwards.

Now the island was coming up ahead, defining itself under the clear sky. At the south-western corner the conical rock Il Faraglione thrust against the horizon. To the north-east, on Capo Grosso, the white tower of the lighthouse was blinding. Just off our port bow we could see the shine of the houses at the head of Cala Dogana. The land to the north spread away in a green of vines, but behind the village the bulk of the mountain was beginning to quiver with noon-day heat. There were one or two small boats drawn up on the beach.

I went forward and began to unlash the seventy-five-pound ploughshare anchor. Long ago we had decided on our 'stations for entering harbour'. Janet always took the tiller while I looked after the fo'c'sle.

31

Now I dropped down into the engine-room and unhooked the lead and line off the bulkhead. We had put a new becket in the eye of the lead at Trapani, and it smelled pleasantly of leather and tallow. There was no point in arming the lead with tallow or soap; I knew from the chart and from the *Pilot* that the bottom was sandy. It was pleasant to stand on deck in the sun and let the lead fly forward with the line sliding out from the looped coil in my left hand. There was always something pleasant about doing a thing with competence—even a job as simple as this. As the line came up and down I felt the lead touch and the line slacken.

'Three fathoms . . . one fathom!'

Janet cut the engine and we glided in. About twenty yards off the shore she gave the engine a kick astern. The anchor went over with a splash and a rattle of cable. That was one of the moments that I liked best, when the anchor went down in a new harbour, a new island, under a windless sky, with all day to fish or work or read or meet new people.

Later we would visit Favignana and Marettimo, but I think we knew already that Levanzo was the best of the Aegadian islands. Wind-washed and sun-burnished, it had a crystal-sharp air—more Greek than Italian. Here there was none of the lethargy of the south Sicilian ports. The windows in the cottages looked as if they had been cleaned that morning, and the whites and pinks and blues of the village houses were sharp and clear. The bare crag behind the village had no shadow now, the sun was high overhead. As the afternoon passed the shadow would lengthen until it stretched across the village, and the night would come down and the oil-lamps begin to glimmer from the houses.

That was a happy week in Levanzo, and we knew we would come back there again. They gave us the freedom of their island—the first English yacht, they said, ever to stay there, and we the first English to have seen the newly discovered cave paintings on the far side of the mountain. On that first day all of the island notabilities came aboard to greet us—the mayor, sweating under a blue suit as he shifted his bulk inside our small cabin, the chief of police, the village priest, the owner of the island motor fishing boat, and the crews of two of the other small sailing boats.

'Three hundred and ten people in the island, eighty families,' said the parroco.

He was a handsome old man, his white hair and lean brown face given dignity by the cassock. Fine hands, I noticed, with an electric vitality so that they kept straying through the air—not just talking with the hands as all Sicilians do, but seeming to draw power out of the atmosphere. I think his finger-tips would have sparkled in the dark.

'There were three hundred and nine last week.' He smiled at one of the men. 'A fine male child was born to Pietro two days ago.'

There was no doctor in Levanzo. Deaths and deliveries were dealt with by the women, with the parroco at hand to deal with the first and last things.

'If there are accidents or grave illness?' I asked.

'The island steamer from Trapani calls on Tuesday, Thursday and Saturday. But in the winter Levanzo is often cut off from the mainland for a month or more.'

He called Sicily the mainland. He called the people of Levanzo 'men and women of the island', and he had small use for the mainlanders, who were 'dishonest and corrupted by many things'. Here in the island remained the old patriarchal virtues. Yet, despite this, there were five carabinieri to the population. (Later when I had got to know Angelo, who ran the village pub-store-grocery shop, and asked why there were so many law-enforcers, he grinned. 'All over Italy the same. There would be many more unemployed if the State did not give men uniforms and tell them to watch other men.')

Later, when they had all gone back for the siesta hours and the hot afternoon had closed over the boat, Janet and I rigged an awning over the coach-roof and turned in. Ripples of water reflected through the scuttles spun gently over the white deckhead above me. Janet was reading. I stubbed out my cigarette as the book dropped from her hand to the carpet. Slip-slop—there was hardly any swell in the cove, but the lee-boards needed hoisting a little more. They were just dipping into the sea each time we moved. I would do that later. There were lots of things to be done later.

When we woke the sun was just going down behind the hill. There was no sign of life as yet in the village. Not even a cat stirred. Over on the point, at the head of the rocks, where the guardhouse and the telegraph station and the old gun emplacement lay, I could just make out the uniformed shadow of a carabiniere sprawled on a wooden bench. I lifted the sacking off the bucket in the cockpit. Snap snap! Our lobsters stirred and rustled. We would have them for dinner tonight.

We had a folding dinghy lashed along the coach-roof. It took only about ten minutes to assemble it, but we would not bother today. Janet did not want to go ashore until the morning, so I would do it the easy way—a way we had, as it were, patented twelve months ago. We had a large papier-mâché bowl (stowed normally in the engine-room), which we used for stand-up washes or for washing clothes. I had found that it had a fine freeboard and buoyancy, and would comfortably hold a towel, shirt, trousers, rope-soled shoes, and shopping bag. For a solitary expedition ashore, all I had to do was drop over the side in my bathing trunks while Janet lowered the bowl down to me. Then, pushing it in front of me, like a water-polo player with the ball, I would head for the beach. There was no need to look for anywhere to change, I would keep on my trunks, dry myself, and then pull on my clothes. A small crowd had gathered to watch the stranger coming in. When I stepped ashore and they saw what the bowl contained they clapped and laughed. Islanders are always interested and pleased by improvisations.

'*Ecco!* The English captain—like a submarine!' One of our visitors from the morning. This was Pasquale, who owned the motor boat.

'That's her,' he said. 'A small diesel engine like yours. A German engine, very reliable.'

His boat had been drawn some way up the beach by a large block and tackle shackled to the base of one of the houses. She was called *Unione* (the 'Union'), because six of the men had clubbed together to buy her. Pasquale had put up most of the money and he was the skipper, but his share in her takings was only a fraction more than his fellows'. We felt her wood timbers, and admired the engine, the tiller, the mast, the coloured picture of the Madonna nailed to the engine-box, the nets, and all the fittings.

The village of Levanzo had one street, one shop, and one small church standing just where the street tapered out into a track that led through clumps of prickly pear towards the mountain. The priest was standing on the steps as we passed, a crowd of six or seven of us. He smiled, then turned back into the shadowed doorway. I liked his twinkling eye.

We made a circuit of the village through the small alleys that ran off the street, past washing drying in the evening breeze, stopping to be introduced here to Pasquale's wife (fourteen stone with a shy smile like a child's) and here an old man who had once sailed in an English ship. He had long since lost any memory of the language except 'Good day!' which he said twice as we shook hands.

'Does wine please you?' Pasquale asked.

'Very much.'

'Then come. You will meet friends from this morning. Last year's wine was a good one. You will taste it and see.'

The store, the bar, and the shop was at the lower end of the street, only a few yards back from the water. It was cool inside, and the flagged floor had a clean, damp smell. The tables were scrubbed and shining. A paraffin-lamp glowed on one of them, and another lamp, hanging from a chain in the centre of the room, was just being lighted by a grey-haired woman in the eternal black of mourning. (She had lost a child some months ago.) This was Angelo's wife, and he himself came in at that moment, still a little doped from his siesta, rubbing the fog from his eyes and jerking at the leather belt that held up his trousers. He was about forty-five, going grey, with a hard-muscled figure and a pair of hands like leather gauntlets. Except for three years during the war, when the Italian Navy had conscripted him, he had lived in Levanzo all his life.

'Welcome, signore. Your lady is not with you?'

'She is a little tired,' I said. 'Tomorrow she will come to the village.'

'Ah, it is a hard life for a woman, the sea. I never saw a woman before in a boat as small as yours.'

'There are many where I come from who live in small boats,' I said.

'The English are passionate for the sea,' said Pasquale. 'Great navigators, the English.'

'And the Italians,' I said. 'Think of Christopher Columbus. He was the greatest of all.'

Now we had all established the warm feeling that comes from mutual compliments, we could sit down and drink a little wine together. It was a clear red, with an earthy tang and a welcome in it that quickly delivered us from any suspicion or mistrust. Quite soon, we were just sailors who shared a life.

'The *Unione*,' said Pasquale, 'only went back into the water one week ago. No sooner in, than we have that bad sirocco and we have to haul her out. Soon they will build a breakwater off the Cala so that we shall be protected from the south. Then, *speriamo*, we shall be able to use the boat all the winter.'

'And now?' I asked.

'Now we must haul her out at the beginning of every October. Often there are good days during the winter, but they do not last long enough to make it worth putting her in the water. She cannot stay at anchor when it blows hard from the south.'

So in the winter the out-of-work fishermen draw 250 lire a day (about two shillings) from the relief. Two shillings, and they have large families. But pasta is cheap and salsa—the red tomato paste—they make themselves on the flat roofs of their houses. *Pasta con fagiole*, spaghetti with dried beans, was a staple food during the winter months. Monotonous but

35

filling; next winter, when we too were broke, we would often eat it. Some things were free, though. Like Sicily, the islands were thick with prickly pear, a relic from the Spaniards, who had imported it from the New World. *Figghi d'India* ('Figs of India')! How often have I eaten them, peeling off the prickly skin with a clasp-knife and eating the pulpy fruit and seeds inside. There was not much taste, but it was fruit of a kind. Like tomato pips, the seeds were undestroyed by the human digestion. By the bare rocks, which serve as outdoor latrines, the seeds of the 'prickly pear' take root, to grow again and feed another generation.

It was time I was going. I had bought a round for the company, and shaken hands with the parroco who had just come in for his evening drink. He asked for a glass of cold water flavoured with anis. Not that he disliked wine—not at all—but he found that, in the evening, the clean-tasting anis best removed the languor of the day.

Pasquale walked down the street with me and watched while I stripped and piled my clothes into the bowl. The water was quite warm, no shock as I paddled out through the shallows to the point where the rocky island-edge dropped deep away.

'Good night, signore. We meet again tomorrow.'

I swam out with the bowl bouncing against my forehead, needing to be retrieved every now and then when it made a dive outside the circle of my arms. There was hardly a ripple on the water, only a gentle swell that the hidden sea was sending round the headland. I could see the lights in the carabiniere's guardhouse and a yellow gleam from the cockpit of *Mother Goose*, where Janet had rigged a lamp on the boom. It would be good to eat now, my appetite sharpened by the rough wine, my body tingling from salt and sun. It would be good to sleep with all the sea air in my lungs, rocked by the easy motion of the boat, at anchor under a clear sky in this quiet cove.

FOUR

WHAT woke me, I wondered, a sound, a movement, or instinct? It was two nights later and we had gone to bed at midnight; tired after a long day's work, I at my typewriter and Janet cleaning and painting the fo'c'sle. Swimming slowly out of the dark fathoms of sleep I gathered my senses. The motion of the boat had altered. No longer tranquil, she was rolling from side to side with a slap! as her leeboards dipped, and a groan from the gaff-jaws as they sidled against the mast. I unzipped my sleeping-bag and reached for the light switch at the head of my bunk.

'What's up?'

'Started to blow,' I said. 'Listen!'

There was a dry rustle over the coach-roof above our heads, where the awning lifted and tugged under the rising wind. Occasionally the rudder would give a deep faraway moan on its pintles, like a bell-buoy on a foggy river. Captain Kidd's cage circled and swung, casting strange shadows. He slept with his head under his wing, but he too was waking with mutters of protest. As I pulled on my jersey and trousers he came to with a jolt; his cage had struck the side of the wooden combing.

'*Merde! Merde! Merde!*' He sparred round the bars, like a boxer looking for an opening.

'I'll go and take a look,' I said. 'We may have to shift.'

The minute I slid back the hatch, the wind and the night air rinsed the sleep out of my eyes. It was quite cloudy, although the moon was still casting a pale glow over everything. Nimbus clouds, a bit ragged, were whirling over the mountain. I could see lights flickering round the carabinieri's guardhouse. The village was asleep.

'I'll make tea,' said Janet, and I heard the hiss and the plop as she lit the stove. The smell of burnt methylated spirit wavered past me, stinging my eyes.

37

I opened the doors to the cockpit and stepped out. The grating was damp under my bare feet—more dew, another sirocco. *Mother Goose* had swung head to wind, and had stopped rolling. I noticed that her bows were pointing towards the entrance to the cove. I hardly needed to look at the compass or at the wimpel flickering and straining at the masthead to know where the wind came from—south-east, the one direction where this anchorage was wide open. It was good holding ground, but everything depended on whether the wind strengthened.

'How is it?' Janet, her head haloed by the light from below, peered out of the hatch.

'Not so good. I'll take a look at the cable.'

Even though there was no tide, we always laid out plenty of cable: three times the depth of the water we anchored in. You got these sudden blows, and often the holding ground was bad, and mostly there was no one around to give you a hand if you got into trouble. It was not like England or the south of France. Most of the places we anchored in were deserted coves and roadsteads. Levanzo was quite populated compared with some.

I hadn't troubled to put on any shoes, so the usual thing happened.

'——!'

'What's up?'

'Caught my foot on the gaff!'

We kept a fisherman's gaff with a big iron head lashed alongside the coach-roof handrails. This was the third time I had run foul of it. Tomorrow I would shift it down to the engine-room. Yes, and if I did, when we needed it in a hurry it wouldn't be ready to hand. This time I knew the gaff had done its job; I could feel a sticky warmness between my toes, and when I stepped on to the foredeck I left a dark patch on the pale teak.

'It is blowing!'

I had been shielded first by the coach-roof, and then by the furled mainsail and the mast. Now I could really feel it. A flicker of spray lifted over the bows and stung my face. That brought me alive. The clouds were coming fast and dense. Sometimes there was hardly any light at all and then, for a brief moment, the moon would ride out along the tattered flanks of a raincloud. I could hear the sea where it beat on the rocky point, a cable or so beyond the guardhouse. The swell was not big yet, but it was beginning to curl and fly where it came round the headland. I bent to feel the cable. All right—it wasn't anywhere near bar-taut yet. We had just ridden back on it a bit, that was all, and pulled the kinks out along the sea-bed. Still—I looked astern—if we should drag, we would be back in a flash on the beach by the village. There were a few rocks quite close in; small ones, but big enough to put a hole through our one-eighth-inch plating. It was a thin skin that had taken us so far, and I intended it should take us a deal further. There was nothing for it but wait a bit, start the engine if it blew any harder, and stand by to move.

'You're wet.' Janet handed me a cup of tea. 'I've put a drop of whisy in it. Lots of sugar.'

'Thanks. Can you find the elastoplast? I've sliced my big toe open on the gaff.'

She went to the corner cupboard where the radio stood, foraged in the back behind the books and charts, and brought out the medical box. It was a fine stout old box, recently reorganized with the help of a doctor friend in Malta. (It had everything in it now, from liver pills to penicillin and morphia tubes.) While I fixed my foot Janet got out the chart and the *Pilot*.

'The barometer's back from 1020 to 1010,' she said. 'But look—we haven't far to go. If it's another sirocco, we can just nip round the point here—round Capo Grosso and into Cala Tramontana.'

'Yes, that's what Pasquale told me. A good place, he said, if it blew from the south.'

Levanzo is about two miles long by a mile wide, and it has only two anchorages of any use to small boats. The one we were in, Cala Dogana, was good in all winds except a south-easter. Cala Tramontana was fine if it blew from the south, but wide open to the north. Yes, it would be quite easy. Some time ago we had got used to this game of hide-and-seek round small islands or headlands. Coming down the west coast of Italy the previous year we had hopped backwards and forwards two or three times round a deserted headland while the wind shifted first to north and then to south and then back again. With a boat that drew so little water as *Mother Goose* we could nearly always find shelter somewhere. 'Anywhere that a rowing boat can go', was my boast.

At the end of the saloon, facing the doorway, were the two bookcases with their glass doors, the book-backs shining cheerfully in the soft light. Between them hung the brass-mounted clock and barometer. The clock said two in the morning and the barometer said 1009 millibars. To the left, and at the head of Janet's bunk, was the tip-up basin, which seemed just a part of the panelling when it was closed. I went over, pulled it down, washed my face and hands, and cleaned my teeth. Now, somehow, it didn't seem such a bad thing to be up and about.

39

'I'd love another cup of tea, if there's one going.'

'Just brewing some more. I'm making toast as well.' Captain Kidd had gone back to sleep. I could tell that the wind was still rising. It made a melancholy piping in the shrouds, and a loose halyard was tap-tap-tapping against the mast.

'I think we'll be better off to shift, baby. We can always potter back in the morning if it blows itself out.'

'Just what I was thinking.'

The strong sweet tea with its tang of whisky was good and warming. So was the buttered toast with slices of dark garlic-smelling salami. We cleaned up in the saloon and dressed ourselves for the night. This time I remembered to put on shoes.

'It's coming up all right,' she said, as we stepped out into the cockpit. Dust was whipping off the foreshore by the headland, and lights were still flickering round the guardhouse. I wondered what was worrying the carabinieri. Then suddenly I remembered the tent they had rigged up for taking their midday meals. It must be a fine noisy muddle of ropes, canvas, carabinieri, and '*Mamma Mias!*' up there.

'I'll start the engine,' I said. 'Then I'll heave in. Start coming ahead as soon as I say "now". We'll drop back quickly on the shore the minute she's aweigh.'

It was one of those mornings when everything is against you. The engine was cold after standing idle for three days. I couldn't find the oil-can to prime the quick-start injectors, and, in looking for it, I hit my head on the sharp edge of the fuel tank. Those are the moments when you wish you were back in a quiet bed ashore, with nothing to do but wait for the alarm clock in the morning. And catch the same bus to the same office? No. It was better to be cursing and swearing, covered in diesel oil (I had turned the tap on a spare drum by mistake), and feeling my toe beginning to throb. Finally, when I had slammed down the primers, she started with a bang and a throb. The water began to warm through the outlet pipes. 'Much beloved product of Coventry'—I patted her painted sides—'you've been a long way with us, and in some strange places.'

I had ten minutes' good exercise on the winch handle, hauling the boat slowly ahead, until the moment came when Janet could put her in gear.

'Now!' I called.

We began to bump ahead through the swell. By this time it really was running, long and white-headed into the shallow cove. We bounced once into a crested curler, just as I was lifting the anchor over the side. I was soaked through, my trousers sculptured to my legs by the wind, and cold water streaming down the back of my neck. It was not that killing cold, though; just cold enough to make one take a deep breath; just cold enough to revive that feeling one had as a child, waking on a frosty morning when every breath and heartbeat was a reminder that one was alive in a brand-new world.

We were out of Cala Dogana now and the swell from the south-east took us on the beam as we swung and altered course. There was a crash from the saloon—something I had failed to stow properly. I went aft and sat down next to Janet. She had the goose-head tiller cradled under her arm with a sure confidence.

'There! You can see the next point. And—that's the light on Capo Grosso coming up just beyond it.'

The loom of the light lifted over the foam-edged rocks ahead of us. The clouds were down low; you could see the circling glow from the lighthouse reflected on the base of them.

'The anchor would probably have held. But it was just as well to move,' I said. 'This other cove may be fun. Might be better underwater fishing than in Dogana.'

Away to the east we could see the lights and the glow from Trapani. Usually the strait between here and Sicily was brilliant with the lamps of fishing boats, but tonight there was nothing. There must have been a gale warning that we had never picked up.

A quarter of an hour later we came round the headland. The lighthouse was friendly and shining above us, but the swell was ramping round the rocks at its foot.

'Now we'll see,' said Janet.

The minute we were round the point, the wind and the sea died away. Only, from far overhead, lifted by the shoulder of the land, we could hear the sound of the south-easter. It was comforting to be in the lee, calm and safe.

'Fine. This is the place.'

We dropped anchor some way from the shore in five fathoms on a sandy bottom. I put out a riding light, in case a schooner or local fishing boat came running in for shelter, and we made everything fast. One cigarette, one last cup of tea, and then to bed, with our hands rough from salt water, our faces burning from wind and spray, and our lungs full of the clean night air.

It was nearly ten o'clock when we woke and looked out to see in what kind of place we had anchored. Cala Tramontana was wind-washed, empty. Nothing stirred, nothing showed in the brisk morning light. We had the whole world to ourselves. It was a curious thing how you came into some port, cove, or anchorage, at night in a small boat, and you had little idea what it was like. You knew how deep the water was, where there were sandbanks or shoals, and how the land rose or dipped away. You knew all that from the chart, but you had no true picture. The first light confirmed or denied what you had imagined. This was a good place, bare and simple.

'A day for a swim,' I said.

The wind, after starting in the south-east, had veered to the west as it often does around there. And the westerly, the *Ponente*, was a good wind at that time of year. It often came along with a warm front, all the way from Spain and the Straits of Gibraltar. We could probably count on several days of clear sky, dry air, and crisp horizons. The winter was blowing itself out in a last shift of vexatious winds, but it was truly spring now. The flowers of Trapani had not lied. Behind us, a hundred yards away where the cove ran out into a sandy spit, there was a long line of grass broken by faint flecks of colour—mallows and anemones. The sky was still a little overcast but the clouds had gone up high, and by noon there would not be one of them left.

A day for a swim. A fine day for a swim, and then to lie naked in the shadow of one of the great silver rocks. And then to swim back again and drink a little wine, and maybe go fishing.

FIVE

'WHAT do you come here and to Sicily for?' asked Pasquale. 'A voyage of honeymoon?'

We were sitting out in the *Unione*, half a mile or more from the land, on a calm evening with the lines going down deep into the darkening water.

'No,' I said. 'We are married three years.'

'No sons?'

'No.'

He made a cluck of sympathy and began to joggle at one of the lines. There was nothing worse than not to have sons.

'Why,' I said, 'we like the life and then . . .' It was difficult to explain, and perhaps I had never really thought it out carefully myself. I shook a Nazionali out of a packet for myself and then handed them to Pasquale and his mate, Pietro. There were only the three of us out in the boat. The cigarettes were badly packed and they had got shaken about in my pocket. The ends of them flared as Pietro passed round a wax match. Pasquale began to haul in one of the lines.

'*Maladett'!*' He unhooked a long green fish, threw it in the bilges, rebaited the line and dropped it back. Just another gar-fish.

I sat smoking and thinking. Why had I come to Sicily? I loved this country and this sea, and I had felt at home here ever since I had first seen it on that May morning when we had made the landings. For weeks, or even months, before that day, I had made myself familiar with the coast-line and with the way the land ran back from the sea, and with the good harbours of the east coast like Syracuse and Augusta. When I first saw it, it had been like coming home, and I had never felt like that about any other coastline, not even the Wash where I was born. That was one good reason for coming here, and I could hardly think of a better one. If a man finds the place where he feels at home he should try to stay there.

43

Pasquale leaned across and looked at my watch.

'We'll turn back soon,' he said. 'We have enough.'

We were out lining, just catching a little for the pot and for bait. This was not serious fishing. Tonight, though, the boats of Levanzo would be going out and the men would be away till dawn.

Pietro hauled in another gar-fish. They had bones like jade and a greenish flesh, and they were not much good. Like so many Mediterranean fish, they were all right, though, if you ate them within a few hours of landing. They didn't keep. Somehow this tideless sea failed to firm the flesh of small fish. Still, there was always the tunny and the swordfish, and I would as soon eat them as anything else in the world. A fresh tunny steak cut and eaten on the same day after you had been struggling round the nets with the big gaffs, and washed down with rough white wine when your skin was burning and your body flickering with tiredness—that was something to remember.

'A little wind,' I said. Cat's-paws were drawing across the water from the south. You could see them a long way off on such a still evening. They were like the whorl-marks on shells, and the ancients had called them 'the footsteps of Thetis'.

'The Madonna moving on the water,' said Pasquale. 'That's what we call those signs. It's the *imbattu*,' he went on, using the Sicilian word for the sea breeze. His service in the navy had given him a scientific interest in winds and weather and he had told me many of the local names. The *imbattu* was most pronounced in summer, when it drew on to the hot land from all round the coast. Usually it set in during the morning, was at its strongest during the early afternoon, and then died away about sunset. Like the *Brise Soleil* of the French Mediterranean coast, it was a solar wind and veered slightly throughout the day as the sun went round. Later that summer *Mother Goose* would often spread her sails to it. If there was no true wind, it was all that a small boat had to work with and it was usually strong enough for a ten-tonner.

'What do you call the other?' I asked. 'You know, after the *imbattu* has died, when the wind begins to blow off the land out to sea?'

'*Rampinu*,' said Pasquale. 'We don't feel it much in Levanzo, but on the mainland it is good at night.'

It was the *rampinu*, the land breeze, which had blown from Erice and the north on our last night in Trapani. It was less well marked than the sea breeze, but the small boats often used it to haul out from the southern shores of Sicily for the night fishing.

'Are you a Christian?' asked Pietro. He was bored with the winds.

44

I knew what he meant—only Catholics are termed 'Christians' in that land.

'*Protestante*,' I said. It was easier than trying to explain.

Pasquale accepted the Church, but Pietro had a cynical eye.

'Priests are like other men.' He winked. 'When they stand in front of the altar in all their clothes—ah, then you think: "That man, he is different from me. He is holy." But afterwards—priests like girls too.'

'We haul in now,' said Pasquale. 'Time to go home.'

When the lines were all coiled down, the fish tucked under weed in the baskets, and the engine started, Pietro began again:

'Our priest is old now. But once—very fond of girls.'

I had heard it already in the village and could believe it.

It was his bright human eye shining out of the trained gravity of his face that had attracted me to the parroco from the start. It would be surprising if he did not have sons in the village.

'Ask me about the other winds,' said Pasquale. He was the captain and he would ignore whatever did not suit him. 'It is important if you are going to sail around Sicily with your lady in so small a boat that you should know the winds.'

I had learned most of them the year before, when we had been coasting down Calabria and the east coast of Sicily on our way to Malta. I was happy to run through them, though, to make sure I had caught the local words. There was the *Sirocco-Libeccio*, that came from the south-west, and was one of the strongest winds in winter. If you were sailing along the south coast anywhere between Marsala and Isola di Correnti you needed to watch that one. The worst wind was the *Gregale*, which they called a *Levanter* further west in the Mediterranean. It often started from the south-west, but if you watched you would see the high nimbus coming over from the north-east, and then the wind would suddenly switch and come with the clouds. I had lain happily inside the harbour at Malta many times during the winter when the *Gregale* was blowing, and when the great rollers were smothering Ricasoli lighthouse in spray.

'Be careful of that one,' said Pasquale. 'Often you will see, just before it starts to blow, that the coast is covered with mist. Sometimes you will see rainclouds lying on the high hills.'

We were coming up quite close to the island now, just rounding the southern point of Cala Dogana. To the west of us the bare flanks of the mountain were bright and shining, but the cove and the village were already hidden in shadow. The water turned a deep plum colour as we passed the fringe of rocks, and the first lamps were coming on in the

45

houses. One of the carabinieri leaned down from a stone shelf over our heads and asked what fish we had caught.

'Four or five. Nothing!' Pasqaule shouted back. He felt about the law the way Pietro felt about the Church.

'All day what do they do?' he asked. 'Maybe they talk on the telephone to Trapani or Marsala. Then they eat and lie in the shade. North Italians! They are not even from Sicily.'

He cut the throttle and we glided in until the bows rasped on the beach. We jumped out and hauled her a few feet up and made the painter fast to the stock of an old anchor buried in the sand. I noticed that the rope of the painter was frayed and tired.

'Far enough,' said Pasquale. 'The *Unione* will be going out tonight.'

'I'm sorry I cannot come,' I said, 'but we leave in the morning.'

Janet had been ashore shopping and we found her in the bar with Pasquale's wife. We sat down together at a table by the small window. A breeze was lifting off the sea and stirring the paper dress of the Madonna that hung in the corner. A small oil-lamp burned in front of her day and night.

'I've been up to the wine factory,' said Janet. 'One of the chaps carried back the demijohn for me. He wouldn't take a tip so I've given him a drink and a cigarette. They've such good manners. It's so difficult when no one will take a tip.'

The place where they pressed and stored the wine was over a mile from the village. It would have been a hard walk with a full demijohn on one's shoulder.

'And then an old woman up there gave me all these. . . .' She pointed to her basket. Dried figs and sheep's cheese. 'She's coming down later and I must find something for her. Not that she asked for anything—in fact she refused.'

The parroco came in for his evening glass of anis and water and sat down opposite us.

'You will return, I hope?' he said.

'In the autumn, Father. But first we are going to sail around Sicily, and then we may go to Greece for a little.'

'You will come back to Levanzo.' He was quite sure.

'I wouldn't mind living here,' I said to Janet.

'Yes, it's a good place. They tell me there's an Italian woman who comes here every summer. She has that small villa.'

It was the only house anything like a villa on the island: a square box, pink-washed, with a small garden in front. The people of Levanzo had told me about the visitor, and how she came there in June with her two small daughters. I had heard that she was a little crazy, but when I had asked about it the only reply I got was: 'She has divorced her husband. It makes her drink too much.' On an island where divorce had never been heard of it was natural that she should be regarded as a little *pazza*. Besides, she was a foreigner from the north, and her money came monthly from Milan.

'It would be a good place to live,' said Janet, 'but you'd need a big library for the winter. Pasquale's wife told me they were cut off for twenty-six days in January.'

How would it be then—when the cloud base was low, and when all the rocky shore was blind with spray? It might be a good place to work, with only the wind and sea at your window. In the evenings I could come down here and talk to the parroco and watch the lined olive faces in the Rembrandt lighting of the lamps. In the spring and summer I would fish. There would be the cycle of the seasons, and the *vindemia* in the autumn, and the fullness of those days in October when the land is rounding off for its sleep. In the winter I would work in a book-lined room—a short winter but enough, giving me three or four months undistracted by the life of the body. Then there would be the six months when I lived in the body only, fishing, sailing, and making voyages to other places.

'You could do it on less than a thousand a year,' I said. 'A house here and a boat.'

'Much less.'

Always do a thing when the chance is offered you. I know that now. But when you are young it seems as if there will always be time to do everything.

Before we said goodbye to the village Pasquale asked us up to meet his grandmother.

'She is an old lady,' he said, 'and she has heard about you. You would do me a great favour and honour if you would visit her.'

The cottage was at the head of the street. Like everywhere in the island it was clean and shining inside. Pasquale's mother, a huge woman with thick white hair and candid eyes, greeted us at the door. Remote from her daughter and from all of us, tiny and shrivelled—a mere six stone at most—Pasquale's grandmamma sat huddled in her chair. She was ninety-one, returned to the foetal position, and crouched already for the other womb. We drank coffee and Grandmamma had some too. She was a neat old woman still, delicate with her cup, and only betraying her childishness by smacking her lips over the dark sugary brew. Her eyes were bright and beady, with a little sharp malice lurking there to prove she still had spirit.

Janet was asking about water on the island.

'There is one well,' said Pasquale. 'It is artificial and was made during the time of Mussolini.'

'He did much for Sicily,' said Mamma.

The old lady said nothing. There was a goldfish in a bowl on the sideboard, and she was watching it as it swam round and round.

'In this house and in my own,' said Pasquale, 'we catch all our water on the roof.'

The cottages, like those in Sicily, were flat-roofed, and when it rained the water was piped into tanks sunk beneath the floors.

'We are not often short for water,' said Pasquale.

'He has a shower bath,' his mother said proudly.

Like most of the islanders, Pasquale's clothes were always clean, even if faded, and I had noticed that he was one who shaved every day. When we had said goodbye to his mother and shaken the bird-like, withered hand of the old lady, he walked us down to the water's edge.

'What time do you wish to leave in the morning?'

'A little time after dawn,' I said. 'Can you wake us when you return?'

'Surely.'

There was hardly any wind that night. It was so still that we could hear voices from the village as we sat on deck. We watched the *Unione* and two other boats putting out to sea. The strait between Levanzo and Sicily was dipping and glimmering with the lights of other boats. The cabin clock chimed ten, each note lingering on the soft air. Time to turn in.

I heard the faint tap on the coach-roof from the depths of sleep. When I had come to, I stumbled up and put my head out of the hatch. Pasquale and several others were grinning at me.

'Good day, Captain.'

Their lamp was hissing and burning, and the whole boat was lit by the bright greenish flame. The air smelled damply of night and the sea. Pasquale pointed.

'We have left a few fish for you and the lady.'

I saw the bright gleam of them lying in the coil of the mainsheet.

'Thank you so many times for all your kindness,' I said. Then I got out from the locker the length of rope we had prepared the night before.

'For the *Unione*—to make her a new bow-painter.'

They thanked me and we all shook hands. I listened as they went away to the putter of their engine, and to their repeated wishes that we would return soon to the island. I saw them land on the foreshore, and heard the sigh and scrape as they heaved on the tackle to drag the boat up the beach. There were no lights in the village, but behind me, over the dim hills of Sicily, the dawn was beginning to lift. The straits were shining already, and soon the *imbattu* would begin to draw lightly on to the land.

SIX

W E HAD the wind on the beam all the way to Marsala. There was
no shipping in the fairway to the harbour and, as we passed the
breakwater, we lowered the sails and switched on the engine.

'I'll get the anchor ready,' I said.

We glided through the anchored fishing boats, schooners, and
coasters, without putting the engine in gear.

'There's a good place.' Janet pointed to a quiet corner, where an old
schooner was lying. She steered towards it, while I pulled off some slack
on the cable and got the anchor balanced on the gunwale. I looked back
and could see that Janet was ready, her hand on the throttle and her foot
on the gear lever.

'Now!' I called.

We were coming slowly towards the other boat, and I waited to feel
Mother Goose check and begin to go astern. Nothing happened and we
continued to bear down. Janet grimaced and held up her hands. I could
hear our engine roaring but the schooner's sides came steadily nearer.
There was nothing for it but let go the anchor and run aft to get a boat-
hook. The anchor failed to hold. There was a crunch and our bowsprit
ran down the fisherman's side.

'What's up?' I shouted as I strained to pole us off.

We drifted away and began to lie back on our cable. It was lucky
there was no one aboard the other boat. She had not been damaged—but
an indignant and cynical owner would not have improved my temper.

'I don't know!' she called back. 'I put her astern. The engine was
running all right—but nothing happened.'

Five minutes later we found the trouble. A shaft coupling under the
saloon floor had cracked into a dozen pieces. It was not difficult in a port
like Marsala to find an engineering shop which could make us another
within a few days. The real trouble lay elsewhere. When the coupling

had broken the engine had been running astern, and this had given just enough impetus to kick out the tail shaft so that now it only just hung inside the boat. There was not enough of the end showing for us to get a clench on it and haul it back.

We berthed *Mother Goose* close in, where the harbour shelved and where the ripe mud surged up like chocolate. I got into my bathing trunks, flippers, and schnorkel mask.

'All ready?'

I nodded and Janet lowered the ladder over the side. I let myself down into the water which was bubbling with marsh gas where our bows had disturbed the mud. A drain outfall led in just nearby. I had certainly picked the right place to get myself typhoid.

'Okay,' I said, and dropped over.

There was about five foot of water under the stern and the job would have been easy if I had owned an aqualung. It was far from easy, though, when I had to come up for air every minute or so. And what I had to do, down there in the dark mulligatawny water, was to try and hammer back the propeller and the tail shaft. I had a big lead-headed hammer with me but I soon found out that you can't really swing a hammer under water. All you can do is get both hands on it and half-push and half-swing it.

'I see the big snag of the Med now,' I said as I was taking a rest about an hour later. 'A tide's pretty useful when you want to work underneath a boat.'

It took me all of three hours to move the shaft back an inch—just enough so that we could get a grip on the inboard end and haul it home. They were three tough hours, with my feet sinking into the thick mud, and my sunburned shoulders rasping against the rudder and the hull.

We made our next port, Mazara del Vallo, at night. It was a bad time to come into an unknown harbour and I had only a small-scale plan of the port. It lies at the mouth of the Torrente Mazaro, one of the only true rivers of Sicily—a river that keeps running even in the arid summer months.

Janet was reading the *Admiralty Pilot*. 'The entrance is between two mole heads,' she said. 'The channel is reduced by shoals on either side to a width of about forty-five yards.'

'Sounds okay.'

'I don't know. Listen, it gets a bit depressing—"harbour subject to silting".'

I was busy steering in on the light at the end of the mole and missed her next words, something about 'black conical buoy . . . red conical buoy . . . an iron beacon'.

'Can't hear,' I said.

'The good book says we shouldn't try and go in without a local pilot aboard.'

'Oh hell, it always says that. Those books are for ships, not for yachts. We'd have paid pilotage almost everywhere we've been if we had taken any notice of it.'

For once the Admiralty hydrographers were right about pilotage. But with all their warnings, there was one thing they had forgotten to mention —in spring or autumn, when the river is full and running hard, it makes quite a current in the narrow mouth. Not only that, but coming in as we were, with a following wind, the onshore swell breaks and turns into vicious overfalls where it meets the river.

We were into the foaming press of broken water before we knew what had hit us. *Mother Goose* soared and staggered like a drunken bird. The wind and the waves beat up a harsh froth only a few yards away. Spikes and broken cement blocks flickered past, and I had to give the engine full throttle to get us through the confused sea. With anything less, our bows would have fallen off to one side or the other and we would have been into the moles.

'Look out!' Janet shouted from the foredeck. 'Come to port!'

The river swung round swiftly into the dredged-out mouth where all the fishing boats lay. I could see lights on all sides, lights from the town, buoys winking and blinking, and a dark lattice-work—the iron beacon— slid past a few yards away. It was unlit.

Before I had got my bearings we were through the overfalls and hurling down under power and sail through a lane of fishing boats. There was a crash and a slap as Janet dropped the mainsail at the run. At the same moment I cut the engine.

'Here! I've got her,' she said, and took the tiller.

I ran forward and grabbed the anchor. Now I was in the bows I could see the two lanes of boats quite clearly. They were moored each side of the river, and it was more by luck than judgment that we had come slap down the centre of them. They were clustered as thick as mussels along the banks of the Mazaro. I let go the anchor and we brought up a few yards away from a long trot of boats. Then the current caught us and we settled back on the cable and were carried alongside the outboard fishing boat.

'Who is it?' someone shouted down.

'Foreigners,' I said. 'We don't know the harbour. Can you take a line?'

'Yes. Yes. Throw us one!'

That was how we first met the fishermen of Mazara del Vallo.

There were no angry shouts and no impatience for the noise at midnight. They took our lines, helped us with fenders, and made *Mother Goose* snug for the night. Then they came aboard and sat over coffee with us, raising our morale by telling us how often they too had nearly come to grief when making harbour.

They were fine men and they did much for us in the two days that we spent there. They would never let us go shopping without sending someone along to see that we went to the best places—and paid the right prices. In the evenings we went with them to the *tavernas* or they would come aboard and take a drink with us. They liked to listen to the radio, but it was difficult to get them to come down into the cabin. First they would look at their shoes or their bare feet to see that they were clean, then they dusted their trousers and did up their shirt buttons. But the 'little green parrot' was a lure few of them could resist. Captain Kidd had learned two words of Italian by now, and they were never happy until they could hear him speak their language.

'Go on—go on!' they would call. 'Say it!' And the Captain would hang from the bars and shout: '*Mamma mia! Mamma mia!*'

Mazara was a strange place, a town dedicated to the sea and to fishermen. The whole river smelled of fish. It was the biggest fishing port in that part of the Mediterranean, and it bristled with the cupolas and belfries of a hundred and one churches. The streets were narrow, and there were many cool bars where they served rough wine and platefuls of pickled sardines. There were no visitors to find the town 'picturesque', or to set up their easels among the baskets on the foreshore. The shops and the churches and the *tavernas* existed only for the men who made their living by the sea. There was nothing phoney about Mazzara, nor about the people. They were as genuine and honest a people as one would find anywhere in the world. Many places were like it once.

When we left Mazara the cloudless days had begun. We knew that the flowers would soon be gone, and the land would begin to shake with heat. Already our skins were darkening and our hair becoming bleached. Our hands had the rough feeling that comes from ropes and salt water, and our muscles were taut from the daily heave-and-ho, and from the constant swing of the sea.

It was nearly two weeks since we had left Levanzo and we were running in on a fine morning towards a small anchorage on the south coast of Sicily. The chart gave it no name and showed only a deserted cove—yet here had once been the harbour of ancient Selinunte. It was possible we might find a fishing boat at anchor—but no more.

I had the forenoon watch that day. Janet was busy on the foredeck, her back bent over the light-weather jib, mending a tear which had started along the foot. Sometimes she looked up and waved, or pointed to the porpoises playing round our bows, or running out to take long dives like torpedoes under our hull. Sometimes they switched to jumping in the wake, and when they rose a few feet away from me I could hear the indrawn sigh of their breathing.

> What dim Arcadian pastures
> Have I known,
> That suddenly out of nothing,
> A wind is blown,
> Lifting a veil and a darkness,
> Showing a purple sea—
> And under your hair, the faun's eyes
> Look out on me?

I knew those pastures now, and whatever life I had to go back to one day I would know them for ever. That was a good thing, that what you had once had you could never lose. When I had come into a little money and sold my flat, how wise I had been to be foolish. I could have put everything into a house, or a business, or into shares that might perhaps have made me more money. In that way I would have been 'sensible and practical'. But now I knew that 'what song the Sirens sang, or what name Achilles assumed when he hid himself among women, though puzzling questions, are not beyond all conjecture'.

Cape Granitola came up ahead of us, lifting itself calmly out of the sea, and beyond it the warm land rolled far away. The next landmark should be 'The Tower of the Three Fountains', and just past the tower lay our anchorage. We were making about four knots and we should be there in an hour or so. It was pleasant to stretch idly at the tiller and to feel the boat going quietly and well under the onshore breeze. A few inches from my shoulder the log clicked and spun. There was the faint sigh of the wind in the sails, the sound of our wake, and nothing else. Of course, life was not always so easy—this morning, for instance.

After we had left Mazara del Vallo we had motored steadily under a windless sky. I had the middle watch and I had hardly turned in when Janet woke me.

'Sorry to have to do this—it's only half past four. But we're in thick fog and there are fishing boats all round us.'

It was one of those heavy sea fogs which you know will peel away when the sun gets up. I could hardly see the bows of the boat, and *Mother Goose* seemed to be swimming not through water but through this strange thick air. The white clouds broke away before the wind of our passing and then closed in as dense as ever behind us. At first I could only hear the rumble of our own engine, and then—all around, so it seemed—there echoed the thud of diesel engines. I recognized the sound of the big four-cylinder motors they used in many of the local fishing boats. Like the one we had lain alongside in Mazara, they were mostly thirty to fifty tons and they could cut along at eight knots or more.

Janet cupped her ears.'You can't make out where they are. The sound of our own engine gets in the way. We were damn near run down about five minutes ago—that's why I called you.'

'Let's come down to idling speed and put her in neutral.'

The sound of the motor faded and we glided slowly to a halt. It was clear that we were in the middle of the Mazara fishing fleet, and we knew that there would be dozens of boats working the banks.

'Here's one coming now!' Janet touched my arm.

The regular heavy stroke of the engine, like the deep snorting of a wild animal, began to approach us through the white night.

'Stand by!'

She put her foot on the gear lever as I grabbed the throttle.

'Ahead now—quick!'

The boat was almost on us, slicing out of the denseness, her bows in line with the cockpit where we stood. There was a rumble at our stern as the screw gripped and the engine roared. We jumped ahead at the very moment the fisherman in her bows saw us. There was not much in it, fifteen feet at the most. My hands were damp on the goose-neck tiller.

'Sorry,' I said, as the sound died away. 'I was wrong. We must keep a little way on her—just keep moving. Starting from scratch like that doesn't give us a chance.'

We had the klaxon out, of course, but it was no use. The sound of it only deafened us and stopped us hearing the ominous throb of those engines beating about through the mist. None of the fishing boats were using fog-horns in any case. They seemed to be ignoring the weather. They had their trawls down, and they were running at set courses and speeds, as if nothing was the matter. They were into a shoal of fish off the point and they were not going to lose it just for a morning mist.

Janet uncorked the thermos and we each had a large cup of black coffee. It had a flat bitter taste after the night.

'No food left, is there?' I asked.

She shook the other big thermos sadly.

'No. I finished what was left just after I came on watch.'

Every night when we were sailing we put up the two thermos flasks; one with coffee, and the other with a stew or a thick soup in it. When there were only two of you sailing a boat that was about all you could manage. Often, just when you wanted to leave the tiller to make yourself a drink or a sandwich, something like this happened.

We were two hours in the fog: long hours of strain, and there was one more bad moment when a boat cut like a razor through the cotton wool ahead of our bows. That second time we had to go astern hard and fast. She had her trawl down, and one of the steep straining-lines went by right in front of us. I could see it beginning to draw aft under our hull at the very second we gathered stern-way and got clear.

'That was near enough,' said Janet.

'Yes. If we'd got that round the shaft we'd have been back for repairs again. For weeks.'

There are bad times as well as good, but you would not recognize the one without the other. The fog that morning was bad, and the breakage in Marsala had been irritating, and our Balaclava charge into Mazara had been frightening. But the quiet morning as we motored towards Selinunte more than made up for them.

'See the shoal ahead?' Janet called.

I nodded. I could see the soft turn of the water where the swell rolled over the sandspit that ran out beyond Cape Granitola. We were closing the land obliquely and the foreshore was only half a mile away. There were rocks right off the cape, and on one of them a heron preened itself in the noon light. The waves were hardly breaking where they made up against the rock, and its dark surface was dappled with bird droppings.

'The wind's getting a bit stronger,' I said. 'We shan't need the light-weather jib after all.'

Mother Goose was heeling gently, and the water was beginning to foam at her bows. The sea put up a wind-and-water music in the wire tackle that ran down to the outer edge of the leeboard. Sometimes it thrummed as we dived off a crest, and at others it made a piping sound like the wind in trees a long way away.

Janet spread out the chart on the saloon table, and Captain Kidd began to scatter bird seed on to it from his perch under the skylight.

'Can you see the tower yet?' she asked.

I got the glasses from the locker and tried to adjust them with one hand.

'Nothing doing.' And then: 'Oh yes, there's something on the coast ahead. A bit crumpled. It might be one of those square Norman towers.'

'That's it,' she said. ' "A low dilapidated quadrangular tower standing on the coast about three miles eastward of Cape Granitola." '

I could see it quite clearly now, the sun catching the ancient stone-work, the land beginning to lift and shimmer with heat-haze just beyond it, and the sea vivid at its feet. There was not another ship or sail in sight. We had the whole of the springtime world to ourselves.

SEVEN

BETWEEN the rivers Modione and Belice, a little east of the tower, we lay at anchor. Seaward, a lone coaster plodded across a barren skyline, bound for Malta perhaps, or across the Ionian Sea for Greece and the islands. The sun was high overhead and we made no shadows on the deck. The boat, though, made a shadow.

I had been down for a swim, and it was then that I had seen it—lying like a dark oval dish on the sand- and weed-strewn floor beneath us. We were anchored in only ten feet of water and I had wanted to check that the anchor was well bedded-in. I had swum back along the length of the cable until I found myself under the strange umbrella of *Mother Goose*'s shade. It was curious the way the whole bottom of the boat was beaded with bubbles—millions of them clinging to her gently rocking hull. I ran my hand along the boat's skin and the bubbles scurried away and then went up to the surface in a silver shower.

We had eaten a light lunch after anchoring—some green salad, fresh from Mazara, olives and fennel and plum tomatoes, a little cold tunny, and some goats' cheese. The wine we had bought in Mazara as well. It was cold from lying in the bilges and had a faintly rusty taste and great strength. We had watered it down, for a strong wine in the middle of the day left you with a head after the siesta hours. And today there would be no siesta for we were going to explore the ruins of Selinunte.

In the violet hour when the land was beginning to throb, and when the circle of sea and sky merged to the south of us in a shining rim, we rowed ashore. Everything was still. The sun had become a great hammer overhead, and the earth seemed to quiver as if an electric charge were being passed through it. There was no one else in the world, not even the drift of smoke from some distant farmhouse to signal human life. We drew the dinghy up the beach, the sharp crackle of her stem sounding loud on the stones. Our voices were hushed.

'She'll be all right here?'

'We can take her up a bit higher and then make the painter fast round that rock.'

The straw hats we had bought at Mazzara protected our shoulders, rope soles our feet, and we wore only shorts and singlets. The heat lifted off the sea behind us and off the pale earth ahead. Lizards scuttled across the path that led up over the headland. They left behind them the thin tramlines of their passage. The cicadas were shouting from every bush and shrub.

Fear in a handful of dust. Stillness and sun-petrified ruins. Here lay the ancient city, running north and south, overlooking the sea and the memory of its ships. Here, then, was all that was left of great Selinus, called rich and powerful by Thucydides, with silver and gold in its temples and a treasury of its own at the shrine in Olympia. One of those sad disputes, with which the Greeks destroyed their promised land of Sicily, destroyed this city. In 409 B.C. Hannibal and the Carthaginian army razed the walls of Selinus to the ground. Selinus, 'City of the Wild Celery' (and we had passed wild celery as we climbed the headland), was extinct by Strabo's time. It had been a monument to the vanity of human wishes even when the Roman galleys swept past that bright bay—where now only *Mother Goose* lay idly at anchor.

A cool breeze drew off the sea and dried the sweat on our bodies.

'More final than Pompeii.'

The ruins at Selinunte seemed to preserve a silence deeper and more profound than anywhere else in the ancient world. Yet always one was aware of a movement just out of sight, just at the corner of the eye, and of a conversation which would be resumed the moment that we had left.

We climbed the hill east of the city where the three great temples stand. High over the fallen columns of Apollo, a hawk wound slowly upwards into the shaking sky. The sea to the south of us was brazen with sunlight. In the shade of fallen columns we rested and drank some wine.

'We'd better remember the ancient gods, and ask for fair winds.'

The spilt wine darkened the stones and was gone in a puff. The stain lingered a few seconds longer and then that too was gone. This was the true waste land. The sound of the cicadas brought no relief and the pillars of Apollo's temple promised no succour. The spring flowers were dying and the grass was already fading. The dusty streets and the doors and embrasures of Selinus mocked our brief lives.

It was evening when we made our way back to the cove. The sun was setting fire to the headlands west of us, and the sea had become absolutely still. Not even a cat's-paw trailed across the purple water. The sea was truly like wine to look at. The professors who had decried Homer's adjective and invented other meanings for it, had never been sailors.

Janet drew her hand back from the gunwale of the dinghy.

'Feel that!'

The aluminium sides were as hot as a kettle on the hob. A small split in the blade of one of the oars had opened into a crack.

'That reminds me to put a brass strip on that oar,' I said. 'I'd been meaning to do it for days.'

We rowed slowly back, and the silence was still with us. The liquid lift and dip of the oars seemed to intensify the stillness. *Mother Goose* lay motionless on the dead sea. There was not a whisper from her rigging, nor a sigh from her rudder, nor a murmur from her cable lying slack along the deck.

The night came down as we sat drinking our coffee on the upper deck. Our legs and arms and faces were burning from the day's sunlight, but a faint air was beginning to draw off the land. It was cool on our skins, yet hardly disturbed the flame of a match.

'I'm going to turn in,' said Janet. 'I've set the alarm for four-thirty.'

We should be under way by dawn and we should see the sun rise to the east of Sicily, and the lights on the headlands go out.

SUMMER

Nunc etiam pecudes umbras et frigora captant,
nunc virides etiam occultant spineta lacertos,
Thestylis et rapido fessis messoribus aestu
alia serpullumque herbas contundit olentes.
                                   Virgil. Eclogue II

Now is the hour when even cattle seek the cooling shade,
when the green lizards hide beneath the thorns; now, for
the reapers wearied by noonday sun, Thestylis blends wild
thyme, crushed garlic, fragrant herbs.

EIGHT

THE stillness of early morning heat. A faint mist, like the bloom on a grape, lies over the sea. The shores of Sicily recede. The towers and spires and roofs of Syracuse fade and dwindle over our stern as we drive eastward. Last night we lay alongside a small coasting vessel laden with pine planks, and the dust of them still powders our decks. It lies like a film over the varnished coach-roof, and *Mother Goose* is heavy with the resinous scent. The cleanness of the morning air and the scent of pine have rinsed away fatigue, and we are eager for the day.

Janet is checking and stowing stores in the cabin. In Syracuse we had topped-up with fuel and water, and laid in enough bread, fresh meat, and vegetables to take us across to the Ionian islands. In Syracuse, too, we had collected our mail, the last we should get before Athens. Mail was always a problem. Weeks in advance we had to let our bank in London know whether to hold back our letters, or where to send them. It was difficult to keep in touch with friends, let alone newspapers and magazines.

Sometimes I thought I detected a reproach in the letters we received, or an implied criticism of the life we were leading. But no one minds being called 'an escapist', and many of the people who were free with such charges were escapists in another way. They could not endure their lives without the escape of women or drink or gambling. There were others, too, who escaped in work, who, rather than face the emptiness of the heart, worked so as to fall straight to sleep when they reached home at night. And if one grew drunk with the sea and the sun and the sight of a sail drawing well, was that more culpable than whisky?

As the sun went higher the air began to stir, first a flicker on my right cheek, and then a steady purr in the rigging. Now we could douse the engine and set the sails.

'Wind coming!' I called.

The wind was from the south-east and that meant we should have to lay a more northerly course than I had hoped. Like most Dutch boats *Mother Goose* did not point well, and if we wanted to beat to windward it meant keeping the motor on. But I would rather take the wind on my beam and add a few hours, or a day even, to our voyage. We had no time schedule, and one of the good things about our life was to know the silence of the sea.

Janet ran up the staysail and the large fair-weather jib. Then we grasped the main halyard together and the curved gaff slid up the mast on its tallowed jaws. Pine dust flickered from the folds of canvas as the sail opened and took the wind. While Janet made up the halyards and flaked them down and set everything in its place, I jumped back to the cockpit and grabbed the tiller as we began to come up into the wind's eye. This was always one of the best moments, when the boat became alive and one felt her lean to the wind, and the rhythm between sail and rudder was established. Within five minutes we had the sails just right, so that the whole boat was balanced like a confident tightrope walker. Then we checked the steering compass against the standard, and altered course to north-east. If the wind held we should come out a little to the north of Corfu, maybe in two days' time.

Janet watched the log for a few minutes and clicked the stop-watch. 'About four knots.'

'We'll do better. It's early yet.'

The wind would strengthen throughout the day. At sunset it would ease a little, but it would stay with us all that night and all the next day. The gods we had remembered in Selinunte would give us a fair wind, and would send us on our way to Greece.

We were taking the same course that many an old Greek trader, or long-oared war galley, must have gone. In an age of rockets and jet air-craft we were making the passage in a boat smaller than those used more than two thousand years ago.

It was late afternoon on the second day when a feather lifted out of the sea ahead of us. Our eyes, dazzled with the shine of sun and burnished water, at first refused to accept it. Then the grey shape hardened, beckoned, and resolved itself into an island.

'Fano!'

Eagerly we hailed our first sight of Greece: Fano, outermost of the Ionian islands, lying some fifteen miles north-westward of Corfu. We had seen no ship, nor sail, nor any sign of life, since we had left Syracuse.

'I'll take the tiller,' said Janet.

She moved into my seat and settled herself back while I went forward with the hand-compass to get a bearing of Fano's steep, left-hand edge. The island was quite clear now as, with one arm round the mast and my eye down to the black vee of the compass sight, I waited for the swinging disc to settle. I could feel on my cheek the cool wind that blew from the far-off mountains.

There was a great feeling of accomplishment when one had made a good landfall and when one put down the first position line on the chart. The sun-sight at noon had suggested that the log was under-reading, and this first bearing confirmed it. We had been averaging four knots across the Ionian Sea.

Half an hour later the sun set and the night came down as soft as velvet. The moon rose while we were getting supper ready, and the sea was a crinkled sheet of silver. We ate in the cockpit under the clear sky, and drank a toast in the wine of Sicily.

'The Greek islands!'

A little later the wind faded to a whisper and then died. We lowered the sails and under our bare feet the deck was wet with dew. Yet the night air was so warm that we needed no more than the bathing dresses we had been wearing all day. Now the silence was broken by the rhythmical plug of the engine, and our wake became crisp and bright with phosphorescence. The lop of water at our bows changed note and quickened as the light on Fano sprang out of the darkness and winked a wide eye at us. A few minutes later the light of San Salvador on Corfu followed it.

I relieved Janet at the tiller. 'I'll take her until I feel tired. You go below and have a rest. Any coffee?'

She put the thermos in the coiled leeboard sheets and I lit a cigarette. The cabin light went out and I was left with the glow of the compass card and the moonlight over the decks, and the still sea. Those were the quiet hours I loved.

It was nearly midnight. I was munching biscuits and touching the helm only every now and then—for, under power on so quiet a sea, *Mother Goose* almost steered herself—when I heard a flutter of wings. I sat up and listened. The sound was unmistakable. I leaned forward, switched on the torch and shone it down into the cabin. Captain Kidd was still there, his head in his wing, swaying quietly to the movement of his cage.

'What is it?' Janet slipped out and joined me.

'Nothing. Only—listen!'

I went back to the tiller. There it was again, a faint flutter of wings overhead.

She pointed—a bird, caught for a second in the green glow of our starboard light.

'It's settled on deck.'

We could just make out a pale grey shape on the forehatch.

'It's exhausted.'

The bird limped aft, hopped on to the coach-roof, and dragged itself towards us. It was too tired to pay any heed to our movements or to our faces caught in the glow of the cabin light. Disregarding us, it pecked at a fold of the mainsail a few feet away, and made itself comfortable for the night.

'A dove,' she said.

We scattered some bird seed on the deck close by.

Janet had hardly gone below when I heard wings again, very faintly this time, more like the echo of wings. Then the second messenger arrived and landed in the cockpit, a foot or so away from me. It was a small bird like a yellow-hammer which now settled itself in a coil of rope and made itself comfortable. Meanwhile, disturbed by the lights and voices, Captain Kidd had woken up and shouted irritably from his cage: 'Pieces of eight! Pieces of eight!' But the two wild birds were asleep.

A small crisp sea sprang up from ahead. It was nearly one in the morning and the sky had clouded a little. I could just make out the mountains of Corfu on the left, while ahead of us the light on Paxos island had lifted over the horizon. It was time to alter course. I put down the tiller and we swung round so as to come under the southern cape of Corfu. The movement of the boat altered as the sea came on to the beam, and there was a dip and sway as her bows swung to the east. By now we had grown so accustomed to living to the boat's rhythms that any change in them would always wake us. It was hardly a minute before Janet was on deck.

'There's the light on Paxos,' I said. 'Not enough wind to sail by yet. We're just about here. . . .' I shone the torch and pointed to the chart.

'Have you seen the light ahead yet?' she asked.

I looked along the line of her arm. A faint glimmer, then darkness, then the glimmer again. We had raised our first light on the mainland of Greece.

Dawn found us both in the cockpit with steaming mugs of tea in our hands. With the first light had come a chill air, and we had pulled on thick sweaters against that dampness which forecasts a blazing day. We had turned north now and were running up the coastline of Corfu. On our right were the mountains of Greece, with the light pale on their jade flanks, and on our left the olive and lemon groves of the island were beginning to emerge in blocks of colour. It was as though a restorer were lifting the smoked varnish from an old picture. The waters of the narrow channel were flecked with *pointilliste* dots of green and white and blue.

Janet went below to make breakfast and soon the cheerful galley noises reached me—steam and sizzle, plash of water and clatter of cutlery —the sounds that meant a new day, and with the new day, a new harbour and a new country.

The cockpit was stained with dew, and the dove still crouched under the furled wing of the mainsail. The other bird had left at first light and had trembled away towards the wooded slopes of the island. I could smell the land now, damp after the night, a blend of earth and pine trees, lemons perhaps, and something indefinable like the memory of a herb garden.

The grasses, the trees, and even the remote peaks of the mountains, were brilliant under this early light. The boats of fishermen were scattered off the shore, laying out their nets, and ahead of us two caiques were catching the wind that had just begun to slant off Corfu. We hoisted the sails (the dove moving weakly on to the foredeck), silenced the engine, and ate our breakfast to the sound of the water as it chuckled under the leeboard.

'Squalls coming.'

We could see them ahead, darkening or whitening the water as they came. The air and sea were disturbed, and the voice of the wind shouted first to port of us, and then to starboard as the squalls dropped off the cold mountains and ran out over the sea. For a time we managed to bear up against them but then, as they grew more violent and more contradictory, we were forced to lower the sails.

'We'll have to watch for those in this part of the world.'

They were the typical island squalls that every Greek sailor soon learns to guard against. The small patches of land rising out of the sea are their breeding ground, and the mountains and valleys provide the spring-board down which they are launched. The worst are the white squalls which whip the whole water into a sudden splendour of foam. Torn sails and broken masts are their legacy to the unwary.

A low tongue of land slipped past, the sandspit that jutted from it showing yellow beneath the ruffled water, and a man waved from the

67

doorway of a white house. The windows behind him were bright with the sea-reflected sunlight. Beyond the spit small rowing boats idled or backed like insects on the surface of a pond.

Kalikiopolu inlet opened ahead of us and disclosed the 'Island of Ulysses'. Soon the grey battlements steaming with morning mist were over our heads: the Venetian walls, the crumbled towers, and the old citadel of Corfu. The harbour bristled with caiques and small boats, and in the inner basin their masts sprouted like a forest. Their curved bows were brilliant with colour. Sailors were washing down the decks, and there was a scent on the air of fish and tar.

'Made it!'

We were always careful not to tempt fate by talking about our destination—until we had reached it. As the dove ruffled its feathers, took a trial walk along the deck, and then lifted and wheeled away ashore, now we could say that all along we had meant to sail direct from Syracuse to Corfu. We hoped—but did not say—that within a week we would sail through the narrow neck of the Corinth canal and find ourselves in the Aegean.

'*Kaleemera!*' A musical greeting from an old man in a rowing boat.

'*Kaleemera sas!*'

The language once spoken in Syracuse and in Selinunte was all about us as the harbour-master's launch came alongside. Two scribes with documents and pens and ink, a naval officer, and two mysterious civilians squeezed themselves down the hatch and found themselves seats below. I produced the inevitable cigarettes, the ship's papers, and some drinks. Gravely we raised our glasses and toasted one another. Through the porthole I could see Vido island, the low hummock of land that guards Corfu from the north, glistening as green as a lawn after a shower. Alongside us was the quay, surging with carts and horses, barrows, bicycles, and the busy figures of porters and fishermen. Everything was moving, instinct with life, and the background of tall Italianate houses somehow failed to dispel an un-Latin air—a bargaining, tumbling, chaffering vitality like an Eastern bazaar.

After the formalities were over and the officials had departed in a haze of smoke and whisky we sat on deck and took the sun.

'Glad we came?'

'Yes. It has a different feel to Sicily, doesn't it? One senses that already.'

There was a sharper, harder clarity in the light and in the people. There was none of that deep, sun-drenched sleep that hung around the coastline of Sciacca and Mazara. This was a brisk sparkle, like the wink of an eye. The mountains to the north were quite blue, and on the peak of one of them a white tower gleamed. The wind had dropped, the sky was cloudless, and across the still bay the fishing boats drew the cool vee of their wakes.

NINE

I T W A S just after dawn when we came out into the Aegean. The dark
mouth of the Corinth canal was behind us, and ahead lay a sea
burnished by wind and sun.

'The first islands. . . .'

We looked at the chart as the rocky outlines of Saint Thomas and
Saint John loomed through the dew-haze.

'That's Tragos . . .' Janet pointed. 'And Molathi beyond it.'

The wind was in the north and we were on the port tack, waiting for
the moment when we could safely turn and run down to Epidavro, our
first port of call. A rowing boat crept round a granite point. She was
tossed up and down by the suck and swell of the sea, and I could see a man
stooping over the oars, while another was running out a line over the
stern. A caique under engine and staysail beat across our track bound for
Aegina. She had a bone between her teeth and the spray was flickering
high over her bows.

'She's certainly driving,' I said.

We passed close by and the man at her tiller waved. He was wearing
khaki battledress and a straw sun hat. On the forehatch a boy was leaning
against a pile of sacks, a piece of water-melon in his hand.

'That reminds me.'

Janet went below and cut two slices from the melon we had bought
in Corinth the night before. It was crisp and clean on the tongue and we
spat the pips over the side with local nonchalance—as if all our lives we
had sailed this sea and eaten melon for breakfast.

As we altered course past the last fringe of rocks we eased the sheets
and took the wind on our port quarter. The nearest rock was less than a
cable away, noisy with sea-surge and the razzle-dazzle of surf.

'It says it's steep-to.' Janet was looking at the *Pilot.*

'It had better be.'

Beyond the rock a beach ran back to the island. Sea birds were spreading their wet wings to the sun, and a man was dragging a dinghy down to the water.

I had first seen the Greek islands as an able seaman during the war. I had never forgotten one dawn watch when the ship had been sliding fast and easy through the pale Cyclades. I had been nineteen then, and I had always intended to come back. It was many years later now, but my memory had not lied. The islands still retained their harsh innocence, as if they belonged to a younger world.

We came first to Port Epidavro on the eastern coast of Argolis, the harbour for sacred Epidaurus. Under the headland the sea was quiet and the small waves were made of glass. Looking over the side as I got ready the lead and line I could make out every detail of the sea-bed forty feet beneath us. It was a narrow passage into the harbour, bounded on both sides by a reef, but I never needed the lead. From the bows I could see quite clearly where the edges of land closed their jaws on the channel, and I could trace our way in as one does among the coral of the tropics. A gesture of the hand to left or right was all that Janet needed to follow me.

The village of Epidavro beat like a heart under the sun. The white-washed chapel clinging to its rock above the harbour was so brilliant that one could only stand to look at it for a second. We made up the sails as the boat settled back on her cable.

'Swim?'

We stripped and dived into the warm-silk water while *Mother Goose* nodded above us. We felt for her all the affection that a landsman may feel for his house, his car, his summer holiday, his ambition, and his place of work combined. She was all of those things to us—that might explain why we were always busy aboard her. Every hour there was something to do: mend a sail, repair a light lead, check a pump fitting, varnish a spar, touch up some paintwork, scrub the deck, polish the saloon, or correct the charts. Apart from all this, we had the steady day-to-day routine of sailing from one place to another. Then I had articles to write, and a book on Jewellery to be completed—an incongruous-seeming subject, but all the better for the contrast it gave.

'We're not idle, are we?' I said as we climbed back aboard.

'Northern conscience troubling you?'

'Not very much.'

As we were drying on deck, a caique came in, her diesel banging away with a reverberation that made her mast shake. She was about forty feet long and maybe ten on the beam, with a patched steadying sail that might have seen service under Themistocles. There were twelve passengers aboard, a deck-cargo of melons, an old motor-bike, three or four crates of hens, and a bearded pirate in the bows waving a live cockerel. The boat had an inch or two of freeboard, no more.

'You have to hand it to the Greeks—they'll go to sea in anything,' said Janet. 'The women too.'

That was something we had noticed after Sicily, where one rarely saw a woman anywhere near a boat. In Sicily boats were for men, and their wives stayed at home or, if they travelled, went by bus. But in Greece the women seemed as native to the sea as their men, and in those islands a man was aware of the sea as soon as he was born, and, when he came to die, it was likely that the last thing his eyes would rest on would be the reflection of tide-rips moving over a white-washed ceiling. The surge and movement round his island formed part of the shepherd's silence, and the fisherman could hardly sleep unless his window were open on the mumbling lips of the sea.

Tomorrow we would leave for Poros, and from there we were bound through the scattered Cyclades to the still centre of the ancient world. But today we would water ship from the jetty and then, after moving back to anchor, we would climb the long spur of land that jutted out above the harbour.

Up there, with the wind cooling our skins, we looked south towards Methana and the crest of the mountains. Northwards Megara Bay was hazy under the sun and Cape Spiri was purple as heather. Eastwards the islands began—Kyra, Angistri, and then Aegina, over whose summit the north wind drove a fleet of cumulus. The wind rocked the olives at our feet, the leaves twisting to show their white undersides—a mimicry of the waves below them.

A goat with mindless yellow eyes watched us from the far side of a cistus bush, and among the ruins of the citadel we came upon the goat-herd asleep under a tree. He had taken off his shoes and his flat horny feet showed he had little need of them. He was lying on his back, his chest and stomach, matted as a bear's, rising and falling. Beside him in a wicker basket were the remains of his lunch—a half-empty bottle of retsina, some small cucumbers, a little bread, goats' cheese, and a clasp-knife.

Two days later we stood into Poros on a bright June morning. The wind was in the north-east, the decks were rinsed and shining, and the land was fresh painted from the night's rain. Around the foothills of the mainland the lemon groves bunched themselves, dark green and dense. The scent of the land had been with us since dawn. It was no sailor's bar-room yarn that you could smell the land when you were coming to it from the sea. (Off parts of southern Sicily, when the wind was off-shore, the thyme scent had sometimes been so strong that we could taste it in our food.)

As we came through the narrow neck of the bay the town sculled itself up a low breast of hill in front of us. The houses were white as icing sugar and the narrow streets mounted on uneven steps past doorways where garlics and salted fish swayed in the sun. A windmill was spinning on the shore, and the southern entrance to the bay flickered with the sails of small boats.

'I'm glad we made it in time,' I said.

'It doesn't look so good.'

All morning the barometer had been falling. The horizon to the north was heavy with cloud and the wind was beginning to come in hard gusts. But under the lee of the small point where we anchored only back-eddies disturbed the water.

'I think we'll lay out the fisherman.'

We kept a large fisherman's anchor for times like this. Not that our C.Q.R. might not have held in any weather, but one felt safer with two anchors down. We lowered the heavy anchor into the dinghy and I rowed out as far as our longest warp would allow, in the direction from which the wind would come. The summer storms of the Aegean did not last for long, but while they blew they made the shallow waters boil.

It was late afternoon, and we were working in the cabin, when the storm fell on Poros like a bludgeon. It came suddenly with a roaring increase in the wind and the whole sky darkening so that we needed the lights on. The thunder followed, and the lightning scissored a sky that was dark as a grape.

I put on oilskins and went out to see how we were lying. The rain was bouncing back off the deck as high as my waist, and the whole boat seemed to be steaming. I went forward and peered through the scud. I could just make out the foreshore ahead of us. It streamed with water like a river in spate, and the sea around us grew first beige, then brown as the sand and topsoil melted off the island. I could not see the olive trees on top of the point, but I could hear the wind in them.

'How is it?' Janet looked out.

'Okay. We're skating backwards and forwards between the two anchors as the gusts come down. But we're safe as houses.'

Something flipped by overhead and splashed in the sea.

'What was that?'

73

'I think it was a house.'

The rain was warm and the whole cockpit leapt and sizzled with the soft water. The drainaways gurgled, and the rain was up to my ankles. I stripped and got some soap out of the locker. It was the finest shower I had ever had, with the rain needling my skin, and the hiss of it in the sea around the boat, and the knowledge that there was a warm towel hanging in front of the oil stove down below. The kettle was boiling and there were eggs and brown bread for tea.

The rain on the skylight had its usual effect on Captain Kidd. He rattled and shouted, swore, turned upside down, and made the screeching-flushing noise he had imitated from the hand-pump in the lavatory. It was warm in the cabin and the rain beat a pleasant tattoo overhead. That was one of the good moments—when you were safe in an anchorage, with night coming down and the sea slapping against the side. It gave you a warm feeling to know that a few hundred yards away the water was boiling on the rocks and the wind was too strong for canvas.

The rain had stopped when I went out on deck to hoist our riding light. The wind was still high, though, and the torn edges of nimbus were skating over the headland. I could just make out the lights of Poros gleaming wetly across the bay, and there was a steamer coming in through the northern entrance. It was the ferry boat from Athens, probably, packed with travellers, and the scuppers running sour from the pounding that their livers had got, coming over with those high seas like a corkscrew under their tail. I was happy to go below again knowing there was no need for an anchor watch. It was fine to get the bunks down and have a night cap, listening to Athens radio, with an old book to read that I had read many times before. Janet's light went out, and I knew by her breathing that she was asleep. I mixed myself another whisky and turned the pages. 'At Damme, in Flanders, when the May hawthorn was coming into flower, Ulenspiegel, son of Claes, was born. . . .'

When I woke in the small hours the book lay on the floor, with my hand trailed across it. My light was still on. I padded out and opened the hatch. The night was still and there was mist rising off the island. The clouds had gone, and after the rain they would not return. There was no wind, and the sky went on and on, with the stars liquid in its folds. The boat smelled pleasantly of damp cordage and drying teak. I could hear fish rising, further out in the bay.

TEN

THE *Mother Goose* soared over the sliding ridges as the wind freshened.

'Shall I give you a spell?' Janet balanced herself in the hatchway, a tea-pot in one hand and a cup in the other.

'No, thanks. I'm fine. Ah—here they come!'

Scouring the surface of the water the morning squalls arrived. Pink shells of cloud were spreading across the north, and there was a green glow over Attica.

'We won't be long now,' I said.

Sliding out from behind Rinia, its attendant island, the granite hump of Delos was taking colour in the early light. A low, crested bone of rock, it began to shine as the sea lightened and the other islands emerged out of the darkness. They slid forward smoothly and gracefully like sailing ships all round us. Only a few hours before we had left Syra, and the twin breasts of the hill behind the town were in line with our spouting wake. To the north Tinos raised its shoulders against the sky and the edge of Mykonos with its spinning windmills was just visible. West lay Seriphos and Siphnos. To the south the gaunt cheeks of Paros and Naxos were fringed with whiskers of cloud. Away over the horizon, invisible beyond Delos, circled the other islands—Nikaria, Furni, Patmos, and Samos— rock and thyme, sage, olives and vines, scooping their necklace of land out of the sea.

The sun was all about us now. The morning light was soft on our arms and faces and the land was coming up fast as the wind piped in the rigging. We sailed in under the lee of Mount Cynthus and found a small bay, just south of the ancient mole and harbour wall. In the clear sand of the sea-bed—only ten feet beneath us—every link of the cable, and the silvered ploughshare of the anchor, was distinct.

Janet laughed as we straightened up from the routine chores of making the boat secure from sea.

75

'Anywhere you'd prefer—Paris, Rome, London?'

'I think not,' I said.

The western side of Mount Cynthus was still dark, but the crisp edges of the peak were catching fire. Just off our bows the ruins of old granaries and moorings straggled down to the water's edge. Fallen columns and squares of marble glistened. 'Misc. Bldgs.' was all that the guide book had to say of them, but to us they were not only a pleasant foreground, they were our main protection from the north wind. The 'Etesian winds', as the *Admiralty Pilot* called them—*Meltemi* to the Greeks—blew hard in summer.

There was a tapping among the bare rocks, and then the goats appeared. They passed in file along the spray-white path, their herdsman following them. He turned his head to gaze at us, and raised a dark hand in greeting. The goats went on up a steep incline of granite, and then only the shiny capers of their droppings remained to show that any life had passed that way.

'Breakfast? I could eat a horse.'

'You did—yesterday.'

The horse steaks of Syra had been good, so had the retsina—in the smoky *taverna* where the fishermen sang, and where the lighthouse-keeper had talked to us of the islands. I had followed the horse steaks with cucumber salad and *loukoumia*, the turkish delight that was Syra's delicacy. The sea wind and the long hours at the tiller had given me back a schoolboy's taste and appetite.

An hour later we dragged the dinghy up the beach behind us and made the painter fast to one of the blocks of marble. The pathway ahead was hard and stony, and the rocks were already beginning to dance with heat. The khaki scrub vibrated with insects and lizards.

'Look at the size of them!'

The lizards of Delos were a foot long, swollen-throated and implacable. They bore no relation to the quicksilver lizards we knew from the other islands and from Sicily. Nothing but a definite hostile movement would make these guardians of the sacred rock scuttle for safety.

Idle among the ancient granaries and the treasuries of states that had once paid tribute to Delos, we smoked a cigarette and looked across to Hecate and Rinia. The passage between the islands was running with pale-blue waves. *Mother Goose* was the only vessel in sight.

'Would anyone miss us if we never came back?'

'I don't suppose so.'

'Couldn't we stay here in these islands?' she said.

'No. I'm a lousy fisherman. And you'd soon get tired of goats' cheese.'

Between the flagstones of the treasuries the grass was growing. The flowers and scented shrubs were thick above the shoulders of the ruins. Here, in the navel of the islands, it was easy to understand why this small bare rock had once been sacred. This was truly the still heart of the sea. 'The Wandering Island' it had been called, for the legend was that Delos had drifted through the Aegean until Zeus anchored it to make a nursery for his children, Apollo and Artemis. In the sixth century B.C., when the cult of Delian Apollo was at its height, Delos and Rinia were both declared sacred ground. Neither birth nor death were allowed to contaminate their holy places, and women nearing their time, or any who were in danger of death, were ferried across to nearby Mykonos. Delos still keeps that feeling of being an island outside of time and time's creatures. But the spring of life, the act of love, was celebrated. Out of the ruins behind us rose giant marble phalli, triumphant over the broken temples.

Hot. With sweat on our bodies, and feet burning from the dust between our toes, we climbed the long ridge where the lions of Artemis crouched. The sky was a blinding blue and the lions shouted into the wind of a new day. Their open mouths, in contrast with their white heads and bodies, seemed to be tarry caverns out of which only the deepest and furriest of voices could sound. They crested their ridge of stone and flinty tussocks, turning eyes of indifference upon the centuries: 'Get out, Alexander! You are standing in my sunlight!'

Near the museum we found the one small bar on the island. It was cool and shadowed by a fig tree. We asked for coffee, and the woman who brought it said wonderingly:

'How have you come to the island? There have been no boats from Mykonos today.'

Janet laughed and made the gesture of a swimmer. She turned to me. 'Tell her we come like Dionysus—out of the East.'

'Not much wine on board though,' I said. 'And we'd look foolish if the mast turned into a vine while we're away.'

The woman spread her skirts and settled down comfortably beside us, listening to the strangeness of our speech.

'We sail our own boat,' I explained. 'We come from Syra. Before that, from Paros and Naxos and Santorin.'

'You know the islands then. So do my brothers. Both my brothers are sailors, and my father was one before.'

77

Even inside the shadowed bar the sea was still with us. It dappled the doorway with its light and spread a fan-shell over the roof.

'There are only three families here in Delos. My husband—you met him in the museum?—he was badly wounded during the war. That is why he was given this position. The other men are goatherds. In summer when the island becomes barren they move their flocks over to Rinia.'

She had been born in Mykonos, and she sighed as she spoke of the olives, the lemons, and the fruit of that fertile island. She remembered the evening promenade through the town, and the lights sparkling round the harbour after nightfall. In Delos there was nothing but the darkness and the croaking of the frogs.

Breka koax koax! Out of the ruins of the houses, the treasuries and the temples, they were calling to one another. We heard them all round us as we walked back to the boat. Out of the stagnant water and the weeds and hollow places where once had stood palaces and temples—*breka koax!* In a shadowed square that had once been a courtyard a frog scuttled out of a dark cistern. His green throat heaved and his sides pulsated. Janet shivered.

'Someone walking over my grave.'

'Mine too. I was thinking of the others who once stood here and heard the frogs:

> There like the wind through woods in riot,
> Through him the gale of life blew high . . .

It was noon already and the sky was beating like a drum. In Delos the very eye of the sun seemed to lean down and make contact with the earth. At this flash-point of light and sky only the lizards and the dry sweet-smelling herbs could exist. The shepherds had long since taken refuge under old walls or in the mountain caves. The frogs still shouted, but they too had retreated into underground caverns and wells where the sun could not fade their shiny liveries. Suddenly—out of this burning whiteness, where it seemed as if we might walk over the edge of the world—we came upon mosaics in a ruined courtyard. The colours were as vivid as if they had just been laid. A dolphin twined his body round the stock of an anchor. Panthers and birds, fish and flowers and leaves, combined to form a decoration as intricate as any Persian carpet. They combined and then sprawled away into a mothy dust of stone where time and rain and sun had weathered them away.

Through all that long day we saw no other life. No ships or sail crossed the horizon. The wind died and the water grew still and purple under the shadow of the rocks. We were alone, as if the rest of the world had died.

In the late evening, when Mount Cynthus was blazing under the last light and the raw granite slopes were turning from silver to gold, we swam in the crystal water. Schools of small fish were exploding under the keel and in the grooved darkness by the foreshore I tried for—and missed—the grey hood of an octopus. We sat in silence over our coffee, the salt whitening on our skins, and watched the moon come up.

The alarm clock woke us before dawn. It was very still and damp as we rowed ashore. When we pulled the dinghy up the beach its keel grated and cried: a clean, sharp sound echoed by the rocks above.

'We'll have to hurry if we're going to make it.'

'I think we're all right,' I said. 'Nearly an hour to go.'

Bruised herbs scented the air. Tall fronds of grass bowed before the squall of our footsteps and then sailed slowly erect again. Snails' tracks glistened on the stones. We no longer needed a torch.

'Yes, we shall have to hurry. I must have miscalculated sunrise.'

Gently and quietly, like platinum refining in a crucible, the island began to lighten under the first dawn.

'No lizards?'

'Perhaps it's too early for them.'

But, as if to prove that the island's guardians never slept, a wrinkled shape faced us at the turn of the path. Not until we were a foot away did it wag a fat tail and slide back into the bushes. To the left of us were the ruins of the theatre, cyclopean slabs of stone, sweating and grey. The path twisted steadily ahead. We were making for the oldest temple on the island.

The rocky entrance was dark and foreboding. Then, as we neared it, the light began to crinkle along the stones. Inside there were bats by the hundred. They drew themselves closer to the roof with a scaly rustle of wings. Their furry bodies shone like mould in the gloom and the floor was slippery with their droppings. We were standing there damp from our climb, our flesh prickling, when a moist light began to spiral down through the cleft above the altar.

'Time we were going.'

As we climbed the last slopes the straits between Rinia and Delos were beginning to shine. And now, at last, we stood on the peak of Mount Cynthus, and all the Aegean was spread below. The island was whitening under the dawn and the sea was wrinkled by a light breeze.

As we stood watching, it began to glow softly, like a pearl taking life from its wearer. The islands were all about us, their peaks clear above the water-shift and the dawn-haze.

There was a shiver on the far horizon, the sun lifted, the light flared along the sea and the night was gone. We were standing on the peak of Apollo's mountain.

ELEVEN

IT WAS August, and we had left the Aegean. The Gulf of Corinth was blinding. The islets scattered along the coast were pin-points of fire. Everything was stark and shadowless, and after a time the light got right behind my eyes. There was a tight feeling in my head and I seemed to float suspended an inch or two above my body.

'I'll make a cool drink.' Janet lifted the wet sacks from the ice-box. It had been dripping monotonously ever since we left Athens.

'It's a good idea, but I doubt if there's much left.'

She scooped disgustedly in the box and threw something grey and dripping off the side.

'The veal. It's gone off.'

'If it was ever "on". I thought that chandler was clipping us.'

I fixed a towel round my shoulders and pulled down the brim of my straw hat. Brown and lean though we were, the midday sun would lift the flesh off the shoulder bones and boil your brains out. The high mountains on either side were catching the sunlight and hurling it with concentrated force into the gulf. The ship's side was too hot to touch and the paint-work was blistering. We had tried every type of 'Best quality, High Grade Enamel Paint' but nothing would stand up to the Greek sun and the steady patter of salt water. The coach-roof varnish, renewed in Athens, was already turning to powder. It was impossible to walk on the upper deck with bare feet. In Sicily they called it the 'lion-sun' of mid-summer, but in Greece it was the hour of the maenads. This was the time they went mad on the high hills, and when blood was spilled as well as wine.

'I'm dying for the open sea,' said Janet.

'Yes, the long haul back. Let's go to Ithaca first. It's a good point for departure.'

There would be a lot of work to do when we reached Syracuse again.

81

After two months and more of steady sailing *Mother Goose* needed a rest and attention. So did my work and my mail: a pile of unanswered letters leered at me from inside the cupboard.

'A breeze,' she said.

'Thank God.'

Between the island ahead of us and the shimmering mainland the water took on the broken silver of fish-scales. Cool air was siphoning off the mountains and over the hot gulf. Beyond the island the sea was dotted with sailing craft—caiques and small fishing boats—twisting and turning like feathers on a pond. Within a few minutes we were into it too, and the sails rounded and took up their comfortable working shapes.

'A soldier's wind.'

A small caique beat up towards us, headed for the shore. She was about the same size as *Mother Goose*, yet we counted fifteen people aboard her. Men, women, and children, they waved and shouted as we passed on opposite tacks, the skipper taking off his cloth cap in a sweeping D'Artagnan gesture as I raised my sun-hat. Their friendliness came out to us across the water.

All day that wind stayed with us, and at night our wake became a milky-way of phosphorescence. It was after midnight when we hauled into a small deserted cove on the mainland and dropped anchor. There was no wind in there, and the night was so still I could hear the drops of water falling from the furled mainsail on to the coach-roof. It was too good a night to sleep below and we dragged our flea-bags out on deck.

'Listen!'

I could hear the dull sourish clank of sheep bells. It was curious how often we had heard that sound in the lonely coves and inlets of Greece, and yet how rarely we had seen the shepherds. Whenever we did meet them, we usually bartered old clothes for goats' milk or sheep's cheese. They were glad of old clothes, and money was valueless to most of them. Everywhere in the islands we had drunk goats' milk or spring water, and filled up the boat's tanks from the nearest old pump on any jetty. We had eaten and drunk whatever we found—retsina, ouzo, goats' milk, citron, broiled kid, mullet, and octopus—and we had never had a day's illness. Yet an American friend whom we had met in Athens boiled everything that came his way. He carried a packet of permanganate crystals in one pocket and a thick wad of lavatory paper in the other.

'You'll never survive summer in Sicily,' he said when we left. 'Why, everything there is even dirtier than in Greece.'

He had wanted to see the ancient world but he would have felt safer back in Ithaca, N.Y.

We were off the true heroic Ithaca two days later. Summer storms were rolling down from the north and I guessed that in the Adriatic the *Bora* was blowing. That was a wind I had no wish to meet in *Mother Goose*, and I remembered from old days in Trieste how they would rig life-lines in the streets to stop people being blown off their feet.

'Barometer's still falling,' said Janet from the cabin.

It was just on the hour and she was entering the log. I looked over my shoulder and gave her the reading.

'Five knots,' she said.

'That's okay. We'll be in harbour before it really breaks.'

It was unwise to tempt the fates. The peaks of Ithaca ahead, and of Levkas to the north, grew mulberry-coloured with clouds and a swaggering belt of rain broke over us. We shivered in our oilskins and dashed the water from our eyes.

'Well, it's certainly Homeric!'

Janet laughed. 'I guess this is the right way to come to Ithaca.'

Soon there was thunder in the north, and rain was driving over the sinewy waves. A ragged curtain of cloud hid the southern half of Ithaca and the lightning flickered. We took a deep reef in the mainsail, swallowed our morning tea, and watched the craggy island come up ahead.

'She's easier on the helm now,' I said. 'Can you take her, just while I change the jibs?'

I had a wet buffeting fight on the foredeck, getting the large jib down. The sea looked very close—it was only a couple of feet away in any case —and I had no wish to find out whether it was warm or not. Bad weather was always a worry when there were only two of you: two were fine on the good days, but sometimes we felt the need of a third. I lashed the wet sail along the bulwarks and hanked on the small heavy-weather jib. Janet was watching me from the tiller, ready to haul in on the sheets as the sail took the wind.

'Okay?'

She nodded, and I swung my weight on to the halyard. The sail soared aloft, gave one deep sonorous crack, and then became tame as the sheets took charge. I coiled down the halyard and slipped back into the cockpit.

'You make breakfast,' she said. 'It's bloody down below this morning.'

The cabin smelled of damp clothes and night-frowst. When it was like this the best breakfast was scrambled egg, and we would eat it with spoons out of the saucepan. Just as I was making the tea we bumped over a curling wave and another cup went. We broke a lot of crockery in *Mother Goose*, but it was better than eating and drinking out of dead plastic or chipped enamel. Besides, pottery was easy to come by, both in Greece and Sicily. The local pottery was good simple stuff, and the designs were almost as old as the Mediterranean.

When I came out on deck the northern hills of Ithaca were pale with sunlight. It was the last gleam before a thunder-storm came up against the wind and darkened the whole island. Just before the hills and foreshore were hidden under the driving cloud I took a bearing of the entrance to the Gulf of Molo. The island was not far away now, but we had lost sight of it. We steered a compass course through the low-flying scud and spin-drift, and the lightning was all about us. No sooner had the flash dazzled our eyes than the thunder spoke, hard on its heels. Sometimes it seemed as if we were right inside the kernel of the thunder-clap. The air roared in our lungs, the surface of the sea was spinning, and all the time the rain beat down so fiercely that it was hard to see the bows.

'Poor Ulysses!' Janet shouted. 'He had no compass.'

'This is bad for the time of year,' I said. 'I hope you didn't see the sea-maiden last night?'

'No, and if I had I've got the reply by heart.'

Theodore, a Greek friend, had warned us about her. If you were alone at the tiller, usually on a still moony night, you might see her white form break out of the water alongside your boat. Her hair would stream off her shoulders and she would rise easily out of the water, leaning towards you on her elbows like a mortal woman leaning on a window-sill.

'How is it with the Great Alexander?' she would call to you. If you made no reply, or if you were foolish enough to say that he had been dead these many thousand years, her grief was so violent that she would raise the sea against you and overwhelm your boat. To quiet her uneasy spirit you must always reply, 'He lives and reigns still!' At these words she would smile and sink back into the sea, and give your boat a fair wind.

'I'd better take a sounding,' I said.

There was a broken discoloured look about the water off our bows and the noise of the sea seemed to have changed. I had just got out the lead and line and was going forward to take a cast when a shift of wind disclosed the opening to the Gulf. The shore was less than a quarter of a mile away and the sea was slashing against the gap-toothed rocks. The cliff-wash had changed the pattern of the waves and that was the sound I had heard.

'Near enough!'

We lowered the sails and switched on the engine as we came up to the narrow entrance. Squalls were whipping off the headlands on either side and not even Ulysses could have got in there under sail. Whatever scholars might say, this was certainly the hero's island, and you could forget about the claims of desolate Levkas to the north. With the rain-clouds looming off Mount Anoi and the sea-surge wild under the cliffs there was no doubt which was the Homeric Ithaca.

The bay into which we had come was large and moon-shaped and at its far end lay Vathi, the capital, just visible through the scud. Now we could see how the island grew out of two mountain masses connected by a narrow isthmus.

'Well, we made——' I began.

Janet put her hand across my mouth.

'Hold it—until the anchor's down!'

Half an hour later we were lying snugly off the small town, a quarter of a mile away at the most. No Customs officers came out to us, and no boats stirred. There were many fishing boats close in by the shore, but the men would be at home on a day like this, or in the *tavernas* drinking a little wine and eating the roast hare that was an Ithacan speciality. As for us, we had a bottle of the rough wine we had bought in Missolonghi, some goats' cheese from Naxos, a salami from Patras, and brown bread bought the day before in Lepanto. We could see flickers of lightning through the skylight and the thunder rolled around the hills.

'Had enough to eat?'

'Fine,' I said. 'I'll make a cup of coffee—a drop of brandy in yours? Then for a quiet siesta.'

All day and all night the storm covered Ithaca. We lay snug in our berth, reading or playing cards, or doing small chores inside the boat. I fixed a washer on the fresh-water pump that I had been meaning to do for weeks, and Janet put a turk's head on one of the boathooks. We were not bored.

Once during the night I got up to check that the riding light was still burning and to look at the cable. Lightning silhouetted the peaks and bare hillsides. The white houses of the village gleamed in the flashes, and the wet shore roads shone like a river.

In the morning, though, it was all gone and the sky was rinsed clean.

'How it sparkles!'

We were taking our coffee on the upper deck and looking at the shining streets and the white houses of Vathi. Soon the Customs officer and the harbour master came out to us. They were friendly and helpful, as everyone always was in Greece. 'You must not leave Ithaca,' they said, 'until you have been ashore in Port Vathi and sampled the wine and tasted the roast hare.'

In the late afternoon, our heads spinning with ouzo and sunlight, we took our departure and cleared for Sicily. Our new friends came halfway across the bay with us, two fishermen pulling them in an old rowing boat.

'Come back again!' they called as we hoisted the sails.

We waved to them as their boat fell further and further astern—until it was no more than a dot on the shining water.

'The wind's still northerly.'

'We'll run down through the Kephalonia channel,' I said. 'If only it stays in the north we'll have a fine passage back.'

We had topped up our fuel tanks in Vathi, but I had no wish to motor all the way across the Ionian. We carried enough fuel for about three days' steady motoring at four knots, but it was dull plodding along to the beat of the engine. Afloat or ashore an engine was only a convenience—and we were in no hurry.

Under the rocky point by the entrance to the bay we eased the sheets and took the wind over our quarter. An old man in a shaggy sheepskin coat halted on the shore and stared at us. As we slid by he turned and sprang up the bare slopes, following his goats. The open sea was marbled with veins of green and blue and white from the wind that had been blowing. The sky was clear, and the shores of Ithaca flowed past. We sorted out the large-scale charts of the Ionian and made ready the detailed charts of Syracuse and Sicily.

TWELVE

W E FAILED to carry our fair wind all the way from Greece and we were motoring over a calm sea when the island defined itself.

First there was a cloud low on the horizon just over our bows, and then the cloud became a shape like an outstretched hand.

'There she blows!'

The sun was westering and the hills behind the coast were tawny like a lion's mane. Off our starboard bow we could make out the foothills of Etna. They crested to the north, and soon we could see the long lazy smoke-trail in the sky. It was some time before the peak of the mountain was visible.

As the day died the wind began to draw off the land and forced us to motor. With her engine turning slowly we could get *Mother Goose* to go quite well to windward, but under sail alone she could not compare with the performance of a conventional keel yacht. That was her disadvantage, but against it had to be set all the benefits of her wide beam and her shallow draught. In Greece we had taken her into coves and harbours where little but rowing boats could go. Off Phanari, where the Acheron and the Cocytus flowed into the Ionian Sea, we had lain all night in the shallow mouth of the River of Woe. We had not seen the grim ferryman, not the shades of any of the dead, but in the morning, swimming round the boat, I had found that the fresh water had cleaned the weed away from our hull. The Acheron had been cold and its sedgy mouth had been noisy with mosquitoes, but at any rate I could say that I had swum in the river of death and had come back to the shores of the living. Not unchanged, though—we were both of us changed by Greece and Sicily.

It was dark when we came into Syracuse, and we passed so close to the old castle on the northern point that we could hear the suck of the swell around its base. There was no moon and the night was cloudy. The town, though, was brilliant with lights. There was a fiesta taking place; rockets soared over the far end of the great harbour and we could see lines of lights and waving banners going through the streets. The smoke of the fireworks and of torches curled as heavy as mutton fat in the green light of flares. There were cries in the night and the distant sound of singing.

How tired we felt! We had been nearly four days at sea, watch and watch about, tending sails, eyeing the tilt and sway of the compass card, leaning against the tiller, and sleeping always with one ear cocked for a change in the boat's sound and movement. We were tired right through, and yet it was different from the exhaustion that follows a day's work in a city. It was only our bodies which were tired, our minds were tranquil and composed. Our sleeps were dreamless and there was a sureness and certainty in our good health. We smoked little, and a glass of wine with meals was all the alcohol we needed.

But the shore was always different. As soon as we reached the shore—even of an amber-coloured old town like Syracuse—we felt angular and exposed. At sea all our defences had been down. It always took a few days to set them up again.

We dropped anchor off the Marina promenade. Even at that late hour there were still a few strollers and they gathered to watch as we motored astern on the cable. We had long learned the Mediterranean way of making fast—common in so many harbours—with the boat's bows held off by the cable, and the stern made fast by warps to the shore. It was a good way to lie, but it meant that you needed a gang-plank out over the stern. There was only one disadvantage—if the wind came suddenly from ahead, within a few seconds you were likely to find your rudder banging against the jetty.

The Customs officer seemed strangely dapper, and his gestures—and language even—a little effeminate after the northern sharpness of the Greeks. His first words on stepping aboard were: 'Ah, what a beautiful wife you have!' and, on parting: 'I will return tomorrow evening. You must see the town with me, and meet my own wife and family.' (He had seven children—five of them, he was happy to say, were boys.)

'Shall we go ashore now?' I said after he had gone.

'I think I'll sleep. But you go on in. Try and buy a few eggs if it's at all possible at this hour, we're right out. Go on . . .' as I hesitated. 'Syracuse is your old love; that's why we came out here, isn't it?'

In a kind of way it was. Half an hour later, sitting in the dark cave of a wine-shop, I remembered how I had been at my desk in a London office, with the magazine cleared for press and the last proofs just gone down on the printer's van. It was autumn, and it was raining. The street outside was misted and my window glistened. I rested my hand on the radiator for a few minutes, watching to see if the rain would stop. But no—it was clearly set in for the night. At that moment my secretary had looked up from her typewriter. She was making some interminable list for a merchant in Bombay who wanted the names of all the British manufacturers of platinum jewellery.

'Just before you go,' she said, 'how about this one?' She held up a trade postcard. G. Venturi and Sons, General Merchants, Syracuse, wished to be put in touch with manufacturers of souvenir spoons.

Syracuse and souvenir spoons—a strange combination! But it brought it all back to me, those memories of the Mediterranean glimpsed beneath the surface of war. It was not the fear that cramped the stomach, the whine of diving aircraft, the hot bomb-scarred waters off Crete, or the noise of guns, or drunken escapades through the streets of Alexandria and Algiers, that I remembered. It was the few quiet hours snatched in intervals of three years and more. I thought of the moment when the sun dipped down and the dark came up with a swirl over the sea. The dawn was even finer: after one had been on watch on a destroyer's bridge through the dull dead hours from four to five, I remembered how clean and simple-fresh the air smelled. Then the stars would begin to dim and the horizon would slowly become a thin band of grey—time to fetch the sextant and shoot the stars. I remembered my first sight of Syracuse after the landings, and that feeling of coming home. And later there had been brief forty-eight-hour leaves snatched in Naples and Palermo—wine and shellfish, oranges and green figs, rockets starring the night over a small piazza, olives in pottery jars, and the sound of mandolin music over the hot smelly waters of the Piccola Marina.

Sitting there, in that small underground bar in Syracuse, I was glad that I had come back. I was glad I had ignored the wise friend who had said: 'Never go back. You're only remembering your youth. It's that—and not the places—which you've lost. What you're looking for isn't in the places.' Well, he was wrong.

I went over to the bar with my empty glass. The padrone was playing cards at the far end with a fat heavy-jowled man whose hands and clothes marked him as a sailor. The padrone looked up and went to the cask of wine behind him.

'Another little glass of white?'

'A big one, please. This white pleases me.'

'It is last year's. From near here.'

The fat man looked across at me. 'German?'

'No,' I said. I was tired of that question. 'No. English-Irish.'

The word 'Irlandese' puzzled him.

'It's an island like Sicily,' I explained. 'It lies off the coast of England the way Sicily lies off Italy.'

'They speak the same language as England?'

'Mostly, but it is a dialect.'

'Like Sicilian,' said the padrone. He was wiping out a glass for me with a slice of lemon peel.

'There are many countries in the world,' said the fat one. 'I have been to most of them when I was in the merchant marine. I worked in America many years. Now I have forgotten how to speak it.'

'You liked it there?'

'Yes—much money. I was in Baltimore, San Francisco . . .' He had forgotten the other names.

I always liked to establish myself when making a new town, and this bar seemed as good a base as any. From a bar you could find out everything you wanted to know—except about antiquities, and I had books for that. From a bar you could find out where to buy bread and fruit and olive oil, and what prices you ought to pay; where to water the ship; and how to get a watchman; and which was the best place for ship's gear and stores. If you were accepted in a bar you would soon be accepted in the town, and then you would learn the life beneath the skin. That was never easy, for Sicilians were a good deal more dour than Italians. They had a craggy obstinacy and a deep reserve which you could not penetrate until one or more of them had accepted you, and had passed on the word that you were not so much *simpatico* (which would have got you by in Italy) but—something more difficult—'reliable'. Once they thought you were 'reliable', that you could keep your own counsel, and were neither a spy nor just a sentimental admirer of the surface of their country, you would see a little below the surface. Even then you would not see a great deal, not for many months.

Over our drinks we introduced ourselves. The fat one was Francu, and my host was Don d'Alcamo. Later I learned his Christian name—Pietru. But now, since he was a man of substance, we were formally introduced. All over Sicily the Spanish term 'Don' was widely used, a relic from the long Spanish occupation. There was a formality in manners, too, which was Spanish, and that certain gravity and sense of pride which the Spaniards called '*pundonor*' and the Sicilians '*omertá*'—manliness.

Pietru went off and came back with three eggs—I had just remembered

Janet's instructions—and a bowl of zibbibbu. Zibbibbu—I had tasted them before, but I had forgotten how good they were, those pale-green kidney-shaped grapes which burst in the mouth like golden drops of honey.

'Sweeter than all the fish in the sea,' said Francu.

I bought a round of drinks and then we had one on Francu and one on the landlord. Most Sicilians are temperate in their drinking, but fishermen and men who live in ports can always use a drink. It may be the salt air, or it may be that men who live by the sea like the shared friendliness that wine brings. The peasants and farmers were different. They were closed in against one another, and suspicious of anything like wine that made them lower their guard.

It was late when I came back to the boat, and only the cats stirred in the narrow alleys. I could see the shine of the lights along the promenade, pooled like so many moons in the water. Hunched in his cloak, a carabiniere drowsed on one of the benches near the fountain of Arethusa. It was very still by the fountain, and not even a mild draught rustled the papyrus reeds. The ducks were asleep and no fish rose to break the silence. I came down the steps towards the boat, slip-slop in my old Greek sandals —they were falling to pieces already from sun and salt water. Tomorrow I would buy a pair of those wooden-soled shoes that many of the fishermen wore in this part of the world. They had one leather thong that slipped across your instep and the soles lasted for ever.

I stopped on the jetty and checked the eyes of our warps where they passed over the bollards. Then I went on board, got out my knife and some rag from the cockpit locker. I went back and put a parcelling round the ropes to stop them chafing. The wine sang softly inside my head. It was curious what pleasure I got out of these odd jobs and how I did not mind doing them, even at two in the morning. Yet when we had lived in a London flat I had been resentful and irritable about the need to change a fuse or fix a light socket.

When I had finished I sat on one of the bollards and had a cigarette. Up in the far corner of the harbour, over where the island of Ortygia was connected by a bridge with the mainland, a small coaster was being loaded. They had an arc lamp on the jetty, and the cry and creak of the derrick came to me over the water.

I turned swiftly as footsteps approached. But it was only a carabiniere, perhaps the one I had seen by the fountain.

'*Scusi, signore*—have you a light?'

He meant a cigarette, I knew, and I gave him one. I was just getting out my lighter when he drew a wax match from his pocket and sparked it on his finger-nail. He breathed down a deep lungful of smoke and coughed. I had forgotten my case was still full of Papastratos.

'English tobacco, signore?'

'No—Greek,' I said. 'We have just come from Greece. The English tobacco is much more light. For myself I prefer Nazionali.'

He pulled a battered blue packet from his pocket.

'Take one, please.'

I lit it from the stub of my old cigarette and looked up at the sky. 'A good day tomorrow?'

'Yes. It is certain. How beautiful a night!'

I heard his footsteps echoing away down the promenade as I climbed quietly over the coach-roof and went forward. There was no need of a riding light where we were lying, and no need really to look at the cable on so still a night. It would be stuffy below, and I decided to haul my flea-bag out on the foredeck and sleep under the stars. Then I saw that Janet had already thought of that. She was asleep on the port side of the hatch and my own gear was laid out ready for me.

When I flicked my cigarette over the side there was an explosion of small fish all round it. The water became fiery from their tracks and the cigarette dipped and bobbed like a float. I crawled into my flea-bag and zipped it up carefully behind me. There was a little dew on the deck, but it would not get cold. It would be good to wake in the morning and find myself in Syracuse. Much though I loved Greece, coming back to Sicily was like coming home.

THIRTEEN

'CORNUTO!' Francu rumbled, rubbing his belly. A young man had come racing down the alley, bounced off Francu's stomach, and run on, without apology.

'May he be horned twice nightly!'

Cornuto was the swear-word most commonly used in Sicily. After all, what worse could you say about a man than to suggest that he was 'horned'? In a deeply Catholic country, where divorce was unknown—except for the fact that it was widely practised by barbarian foreigners—a man's honour was still bound up with that of his wife. Cuckoldry was the source of most of the jokes in the cafés, bars, and men's clubs. To 'put horns' on another man was a real achievement, an achievement because it was dangerous, and because it really did lower the man concerned in the eyes of his fellows. An acquaintance of mine in Palermo had fought two duels over the honour of his wife. But duelling was illegal, and it was also strictly upper-class. The working-class husband tended to avenge his honour with a knife-thrust—usually a good deal more damaging than the 'honourable' duel, where people rarely got hurt.

There was some blasphemous swearing in Sicily, but nothing like the blasphemy of the Florentines. Here, it was a man's honour which you impugned if you wished to get at him; and his honour meant his wife, his family, and, of course, his mother.

In England 'bastard' can be a cheery greeting among the educated (who are all quite confident that they know who their fathers are), but among matelots and working-class men 'bastard' usually leads to a fight. It is curious how much our swearing has changed over the centuries. To Shakespeare and his contemporaries Francu's use of *cornuto* would have seemed quite normal.

The cuckoo then, on every tree,
Mocks married men; for thus sings he,
Cuckoo:
Cuckoo, cuckoo: O word of fear,
Unpleasing to the married ear!

But 'cuckold' means little nowadays in western Europe, for contraceptives and equal rights for women have devalued their 'quaint honour'. Then again, swearing by the pox—still heard in Sicily where medicine has made less headway—has meant little in England since the eighteenth century, and almost nothing since penicillin. Even the old medical student's joke, 'One night with Venus and seven years with Mercury,' has lost its point.

I was thinking about this as Francu and I walked down to the market. We went past the temple of Diana, on over the bridge, and stopped to stare at the fishing boats gathered in the small harbour. They had the eyes painted on their bows and the high stempiece one finds in that part of the world. In the museum a few yards away I had seen similar boats on fragments of Greek pottery. Little changed in this sea. That was why life had a feeling of continuity which it had long since lost in other countries. Whatever the priests might say, men here believed with Homer:

As is the life of leaves, so is that of men. The wind scatters the leaves to the ground: the vigorous tree puts forth others, and they grow in the spring season. Soon one generation of men comes and another ceases.

A fisherman with the collapsed nose-bridge of hereditary syphilis called out to us.

'Do you want to buy any fish?' Francu asked.

'I'd like a few mullet if he has them.'

We went down to the worn old steps beside the bridge and the man found me four mullet and wrapped them in a page of the *Giornale di Sicilia*. He had come in less than an hour ago, and one of the fish still quivered. It had not been a good night's fishing. He had been a long way out, past Cape Murro di Porco, and the offshore wind had taken him too far from the banks. He was away now to get some sleep. I paid him—a few lire more than he asked—which was still cheaper than the fish would have been in the market. Anyway, what he was doing was technically illegal, for all fish were supposed to be sold direct to the market. Fishermen were not allowed to be their own retailers, and in some fishing

94

ports you were not supposed to be able to buy fish until it had been sent inland to the central market of the province—and then come back again for distribution.

'*Sifilitico*,' said Francu, tapping his nose as we mounted the steps. This was merely a statement and not derogatory.

We saw Janet a long way off through the market. She was followed as usual by half a dozen young men with sheep's eyes. That was one of the most trying things for a foreign woman in this land. Even if her Italian was as good as Janet's, and even if she was as careful to dress in a way that could not offend local susceptibilities, she would still be followed by amorous youths. They disappeared as Francu and I came up, all except one and he was carrying a pile of parcels.

'Thanks for the relief of Mafeking,' she said. 'Still, it does make you feel good. Excellent for the morale, even if the suggestion that one's on the batter is a bit insulting.'

'How about *him?*' I said.

'Oh, that's Raimondo. He attached himself to me as soon as I left the boat. He's quite nice. Besides, look at all the stuff he's carrying.'

Francu knew him. He was the nephew of a cousin or something complicated. He called Francu 'uncle' and was very polite. In Syracuse you found the best manners in Sicily and you also found the best-looking people. Raimondo was very typical: fine brown eyes and a full mouth, dark curly hair and a straight nose: almost classical Greek features and forehead. After two thousand years of conquest and inter-marriage with so many nations it was impossible to believe that any of the old Greek strain still persisted in this part of Sicily. It was curious, though, how much better-looking the east-coast Sicilians were. Along the southern coast you got much ugliness and a good deal of dark Moorish stock. In Palermo and on the northern coast they were a mixture of every race. It was only in Syracuse, and one or two of the neighbouring ports like Augusta and Riposto, that this particular strain predominated. The men were certainly handsome, and some of the young women had the features and the carriage of Nausicaa. But that was when they were sixteen. By the time they were thirty, pasta, child-bearing, and the hot sun had reduced them to sad overblown shapes. Life in the south maintains its classic rigour: short, sweet spring; long, fertile summer; brief autumn; and briefer winter.

Francu and Raimondo came back with us to the boat. On the way we stopped at a stationer's and bought a pack of Sicilian playing cards. They were narrower than the English ones, and I liked their antique figures and the different symbols which gave them a mediaeval quality—*coppe, spade, ma₃₃e, and denari*—cups, spades, clubs, and money.

'We'll show you how to play Briscola,' said Francu.

It was a simple gambling game, rather like 'Snap', and I had often watched the fishermen playing it in the bars. They put great vehemence into their calling and sweated heavily over the results. If you had not known what it was all about, you would have thought that at any minute their knives would be out.

It was hot now in this last week of August. The still half-moon of the harbour trembled with heat. The land behind it quivered, and only the heights of Epipolae and the Hyblaean mountains, blue in the distance, suggested that anywhere in the world there was coolness and a fresh breeze. We sat in the cockpit under the awning and played Briscola for cigarettes. I lost, Janet won a little, and Francu won nearly a whole pack.

At noon Francu went back to his home on the east side of Ortygia, back to the teeming narrow alleys where the sea breeze rustled through the washing overhead. Raimondo went with him. I would see them again in the evening for I was going out fishing in Francu's boat, and Raimondo had been asked to make one of the crew. Janet would not come: the men were embarrassed by women in a boat.

We had long ago learned to conform to the siesta habit. In those blinding hours of summer there is nothing to do from midday until four in the afternoon but sleep like a lizard under a stone. We ate the mullet and a good green salad, and drank some of the white wine from Pietru's tavern. Under the awning on the foredeck, if you lay still, with only the minimum of clothes on, you could feel a faint damp air rustle over your body. It was just enough to stop the sweat breaking out, but not enough to give you a chill if you went to sleep.

Janet woke me with a Campari-soda with ice in it.

'Tea-time,' she said. We kept the old hours, but tea was unthinkable in this heat. Still, we had cucumber sandwiches, just as if we had been in England, listening to the tonk-tonk of tennis on a green lawn.

'Get up, you lazy brute. If we're going to take a look at the Ciane before you go out fishing we ought to start.'

'We're not going out till nearly midnight,' I said. 'There's plenty of time.'

The Ciane River lies on the far side of the harbour. It took us nearly an hour to get there, rowing, and with an occasional puff of wind lifting the dinghy's sail. Even in the late afternoon it was blinding out in the middle of the bay and I was glad when we reached the eucalyptus trees that fringed the river mouth. The scent of them was very strong on the hot air. Then, as I rowed up the narrowing stream, the coolness of all the lemon groves in that fertile delta came over us like a cloud shadowing the sun. Soon we were moving through the dense stems of papyrus and the muddy jungle smell was all about us. We might have been in South America, and it was difficult to recall the classic columns in the old town, or the great bowl of the Greek theatre on the slope overlooking the harbour.

'*Primitivo*,' said Janet. And then, 'Look at those dragon-flies!'

There were dozens of them hovering in the hot steamy air. Their wings glittered and they shifted like sparks on an apple-log in a fire. Something jumped with a splash into the water ahead of us, and then we came out into a cool basin where the Ciane rises. That basin of bubbling water was unique in summer Sicily. Fish were rising and papyrus swayed all around. To come on such coolness out of the burning land and the brilliant shine of the harbour was to understand the Greek legends of the fountain nymphs. Water is sacred in those hot lands, and the Testa della Pisma, the river's head, where we now rested on our oars, still holds a goddess.

'We ought to bathe here.'

The water was almost cold, the first cold water we had felt on our bodies for many months. It erased the fatigue of the hot day and made our eyes sparkle. Our brains were cleared of that lethargy and ennui which the midsummer sun brings down.

'God, that was good!' I said, as we rowed briskly downstream. The fresh water beaded our hair and dried on our bodies. 'I wonder if that makes us nympholept.'

I had come across the word in a book recently and had looked it up: 'A person inspired by violent enthusiasm, especially for an ideal. '

'I guess we were already.'

'Nympholepsy is fatal. It unfits you for the world.'

That night Francu and Raimondo came chugging alongside *Mother Goose*. Francu's boat was about twenty foot long, with a short mast and a lateen sail. A small Italian diesel throbbed away under a box amidships. Janet passed me down some sandwiches, a thermos of coffee, and a flask of brandy—my contribution to the night.

We went out through the narrow channel past Castello Maniace, sombre and peaceful under the velvet sky. I tried to tell them how it was here that the last desperate fling of the Athenian expedition had come to nothing. It was just here, where the water rolled up in a slow swell from the south, that the galleys had failed to break through the boats moored by the Syracusans across the entrance. It was on this strip of water, where the three of us now puttered out for a night's fishing, that the Athenian dream had finally broken. The sound of that day's fighting, when the Athenian soldiers had watched the defeat of their fleet from the slopes of Maddalena peninsula, still echoed through the world.

'Yes, of course,' said Francu. 'I remember the landings——'

I looked startled.

'Of course I remember the landings down the coast.' He spat over the side. 'Soon after them, the Americans come into town, and the Germans go.'

When I was in Sicily I never said that I too had been in 'the landings down the coast', and anyway I was not talking of that war. But there had been so many invaders of Sicily that they had all become muddled up in the native memory. No Sicilian could remember much of his history, except that the Moors had held the island for a long time.

'They were not Christians,' said Raimondo. He had been trying to follow my story of the Athenian expedition.

'No, it was before Christ,' I said.

'We learned about it at school.'

Francu came out of his reverie over the tiller.

'Of course they were Christians,' he said. 'I know, I've been there. There are many Christians in America. There are Protestants as well, but there are many Christians—from Sicily and Italy mostly.'

We turned north once we were clear of the harbour and went up past the town towards the banks that lie off Panagia point. There were lots of lights along the east side of Syracuse, and Francu tried to show me where his house lay in relation to a neon sign and a cluster of street lamps.

There were many boats working the banks ahead of us, and we could see their lamps lifting and dipping in the slow swell. Soon we would light our own and begin to fish.

'There will be a breeze,' said Francu.

A faint flicker stirred the water.

'I will go out to sea with the engine. In the morning when the breeze comes off the mountain, we shall be able to sail back.'

Like most of the fishermen he did not use the name 'Etna'. It was always 'the mountain', or sometimes the hybrid Latin-Arabic word, 'Mongibello'. People who live under the shadow of great volcanoes do not use their names very much. It would be a kind of discourtesy to do so —a tempting of fate.

We went seaward and a little eastward of most of the fleet. I could still see the lights of Syracuse and those of Augusta to the north. Inland there was a twinkle from many hill villages.

Francu was right, the breeze was coming. It brought the land with it —fruit and hot earth and all the Sicilian summer. He wrinkled his nose and smiled at me in the bright light of the acetylene lamp.

'The wind off the island smells very sweet at nights.'

AUTUMN

Quae tibi, quae tali reddam pro carmine dona?
nam nequeme tantum venientis sibilus Austri
nec percussa iuvant fluctu tam litora, nec quae
saxosas inter decurrunt flumina valles.

Virgil. Eclogue V

What gift can I bring, what return can I make for a song
such as yours?—sweeter to me even than the sigh of the
South Wind coming, or the shores beaten by the surf, or
the sound of the streams as they run through the rocky
valleys.

FOURTEEN

I T WAS NOON. The waves were feathered with white and *Mother Goose* surged and trembled as she flew along under a brisk north-easter. Although the sun was high overhead, there was a fresh edge to the air, a hint of approaching autumn. The sky was a hard, cloudless blue and the coast and the inland hills stood out in sharp scraped lines. The Gulf of Augusta lay on our port beam and the white village was distinct against the bare land. We were bound up the coast for Riposto, Catania, and Messina—the three other harbours of eastern Sicily.

'There's thunder about,' said Janet. 'I've got a tight band across my head.'

'I wouldn't be surprised. It's the time of the year for it.'

I looked at *Mother Goose*'s brightwork and varnish and new paint sparkling in the sunlight. We had spent nearly a week in Syracuse making good the ravages of summer. Our voyage to Greece and back had been several thousand miles alone, and the past eight days in Syracuse was the longest time we had spent in any port since the year began.

'That was a good piece of stuff old Francu found for the jib sheets,' she said.

'Yes. I wonder where it was knocked off. You don't see much nylon about in this part of the world.'

We heeled and lifted over a long foaming crest. The leeboard rolled out and came back with a clonk against the cheek block. The log flicked round and our wake drew a sword over the sea.

'I could do with a drink,' I said.

'I'm just fixing one. Gin and Campari do you?'

'What better? We can get some more ice in Riposto so there's no point in hoarding it.'

The wind began to fade in the early afternoon, just as we were drawing level with Cape Campolato to the north of Augusta. Over the barren headland the sky began to bloom, and took on a rich violet shade. There was a tense feeling in the air.

'You were right,' I said. 'Take a look over the land.'

Janet tapped the barometer as she came out.

'It's just dropped about a quarter of an inch.'

The storm was coming up fast against the wind, its darkness intensified by the bleached shoulders of the cape. The long fertile plain of Catania was disappearing under a cloak of rain. It looked like a typical Mediterranean thunder-storm, and it would be fierce while it lasted.

'We'd better get the sails off her. It's coming up at a rate.'

With only two of us aboard we were cautious about bad weather. It was easy enough to hold on to canvas if you had a large crew, but it could be dangerous when you were shorthanded.

'Stand by!'

I took the turns of the halyards and began to lower the mainsail. Janet grabbed the folds as they slid on to the boom. When it was all down we got the canvas tiers quickly round the sail. Then it was the turn of the jib.

'Let's not take it below,' she said. 'We're going to get buckets of rain. This should wash some of the salt out of it.'

We spread the big fair-weather jib across the foredeck and passed lashings over it so that no gust of wind could get underneath and tear it free. *Mother Goose* idled to a standstill and began to roll in on the onshore swell. There was lightning over the land and the hollow rumble of thunder.

'Better start the engine—quick!'

A fishing boat was coming towards us from the land. Her crew were lowering her lateen sail and the boat was booming along before a wind that had not yet reached us. The cape had disappeared. A few wild gusts, advance guard of the storm, rattled through the rigging. We turned under power and headed towards the dark cloud.

'We'll do better to keep pointed into it,' I said.

That way we would be through it quicker and, besides, there was no point in running before it. We didn't want to go out to sea.

A few minutes later it was on us. The rain came down in long whip-like lashes and the wind was gale force in the squalls. At three-quarters full power we were just managing to stem the weather. There was no point in putting on oilskins: after a few seconds my shirt and trousers were soaked through and I stripped off.

'They pay a quid for a skin massage like this in Turkish baths!' I said.

After the hot days the spears of rain were as good on the skin as a lemon ice after a siesta.

When the eye of the storm went overhead I had to put the engine up to full power. The swell from the day's wind had long since become a jumble of turning and breaking waves. Even at full power it was almost impossible to keep the boat head to wind, and then the squalls began to whip round us from all sides. First we would fall off to port, and then to starboard. The old boat was jumping and bucking like a young stallion. Captain Kidd was shouting down below and I heard Janet curse as a long-drawn sigh, tinkle, and crash showed that something had bounced out of the galley locker and broken. There was nothing for it now but to turn with the storm and run before it. We cut the engine right down, so that we just had steerage way, and swung her round in the lull between two waves.

'1625', the log-book reads. 'Impossible to keep boat head to wind and we had to run her off. The wind was about forty miles an hour by our pocket anemometer. More in the gusts.' The crests were flying headlong from the waves. Dust and sand from the shore whirled in our faces and turned to mud on the decks.

Five minutes later the torn coat-tails of the thunder-storm flickered over our heads and the barometer gave a sharp bound upwards. The sun was bright over Cape Campolato, and a tower on the point gleamed as if newly white-washed. In the far distance the hills had a sharp clarity as though the wind and rain had swept and dusted them, brooming away the fatigue of summer.

'It's chaos below.' Janet came up with a lighted cigarette, a towel, and a dry pair of trousers. I wiped my face and put the cigarette between my lips. My mouth was rinsed with rain, my lungs full of the wild air, and the tobacco had a real taste.

'What broke?' I said.

'You may well ask "what broke"! There's a whole jar of salsa all over the deck . . . I've trodden it into the carpet and it's splashed all over the panelling and the bulkheads.'

I looked past her into the cabin. It was like a battlefield. The dark-red tomato-paste had shot over everything.

'It's not only salsa,' she said. Some of it's genuine Bedouin gore. I cut my finger trying to pick up the pieces.'

'Let's go in and anchor. We can't clear up that mess at sea. Besides, Porto Brucoli's only just round the point here. We can go on up the coast tomorrow.'

As quickly as it had come up the cross-sea subsided. The rain had killed the swell and we motored over a pale-blue calmness. Fish were rising ahead of us, so I eased the throttle and got out a couple of mackerel lines. I had them made up round rough slabs of cork, but they were always devils to handle. As usual, I managed to get a hook into one of my fingers. I put the lines out through the port and starboard fairleads on the quarter, and cut the engine down until we were gliding along at a little over a knot.

We were pretty well into the shoal now and if we were going to get fresh fish for supper it would be soon. Then the mackerel began to hit the lines. Janet hauled in on the port side—four on that. It was always a muddle in that small cockpit, with two of you, and the lines coming in and the nylon trace kinking and twisting the hooks all over the place. We got the fish off, sorted out the line and paid it out again, then I turned to the other one. There were three of them on it, good-sized fish and firm.

'We're in luck today.'

Sometimes we could prowl along for hours and get nothing, even though we knew there were fish all round us.

'Making up for that thunder-storm, and the spilt salsa,' I said.

We took three more and called it a day. The land was close and I never liked being cumbered up with lines and hooks when making a new place. Sometimes you would get squalls when you were least expecting them, and once we had nearly run aground off a point that was marked as 'steep-to'. Most of the Mediterranean was as well charted as Piccadilly Circus, but there were a few places—along the northern shores of the Gulf of Patras for one—where a ship's boat could still put in a useful day's survey work.

Porto Brucoli is a small village in the south-western corner of a cove, tucked away behind Cape Campolato, and a little north of Augusta. Janet looked it up in the *Pilot*.

'Can you see the castle?' she asked.

'Yes. A bit dilapidated—three or four towers.'

'That's it. It stands to the north of the village.'

I got out the binoculars. 'I can see the entrance now. It looks a good spot. It'll be open to the north, though.'

We dropped anchor in three fathoms quite close to the shore, a hundred yards away from a fifty-ton fishing boat. There were a number of rowing boats drawn up on the beach, bright against the brown of the land, and the village that clustered around the head of the cove was white-wash, and pink-wash, and blue. We could see people moving along the front, and the gleam of their faces as they turned to stare at us. Even in England Dutch boats are fairly uncommon, but in Sicily the strange fans of our leeboards and the tubby shape of our hull were unique. In some of the small ports and anchorages they had never even seen a yacht before.

A few minutes later a rowing boat came out with the Port Commandante aboard, pulled by two fishermen. While he was taking a whisky down below, and admiring the panelling and Captain Kidd, and commenting on the bravery of a woman living aboard a small boat, I heard other boats bumping alongside. I went up and found that we were surrounded. The whole village, it seemed, had come out to have a look at *Mother Goose*. The air had become still and heavy with heat, and there was a humidity which I did not like. I pointed to the sky and one of the fishermen shook his head.

'*Tempo cattivo, signore*.'

It looked as if we were in for one of those breaks in the weather which often occur in early September. The summer went out with a roll of drums and then the weather settled down again for two months or more—the golden autumn days, next to spring the most beautiful in the island.

'*Tempo cattivo*,' said the commandante as he was getting into his boat to be pulled back ashore. 'But don't worry. You are all right here for the night. In the morning we will come and see you again. It would be better if you anchored a little further out, in case the wind should go round to the north. If you should need any help in the night just fetch Antonio here——' he pointed to the bowman. 'He sleeps on the foreshore in his boat.'

Antonio was almost black from the sun, with grizzled hair and a gap-toothed smile. He tapped his chest and pointed to a large rowing boat on the edge of the shore. He slept aboard it under a canvas awning. He would hear if the wind rose and would come out if we needed to shift our berth.

'I sleep lightly, signore. If you call out, even if I do not hear you, my dog will. He will waken me with his barking.'

We were tired after the long day which had started with sun and heat, gone on to wind, rain, and sudden storm, and ended in thundery tension.

The mackerel were fine, done in oatmeal and washed down with some of the white wine from Syracuse. The last thing I remembered was the growl of the anchor chain as it eased itself to and fro in the hawsepipe. The barometer was low and the wind came from the south-west.

FIFTEEN

'TROMBA MARINA!' cried Antonio.

'*Che——?*'

'*Tromba marina!*'

He and his two sons had been sitting with us on the foredeck of *Mother Goose*. Now they were all on their feet, staring seaward.

'We must look to the boats,' he said.

The three of them disappeared over the side and I watched them row rapidly inshore.

'What?'

I had not caught the word, but it was too late to ask now. I gazed out over the grey windswept sea to the north. Just to the left of the small mole a dark cloud hung down over the water. Something like a ragged coat-sleeve was flickering between the cloud base and the sea.

'*Tromba marina.*' Janet came up with the dictionary. 'A waterspout.'

'That's all we needed,' I said. The weather had really broken in the last twenty-four hours.

I looked back at the beach and saw Antonio and his sons taking their boat up at a run. Other fishermen were busily securing boats, lashing down canvas coverings, and stowing away sails that had been hung out to dry. The way the wind was, it looked as if the spout might pass clean across the harbour.

'It's coming this way all right,' said Janet.

When Antonio had first spotted it the cloud had been two or three miles away, but it was coming up at such a speed that already we could see every detail of it. The ragged arm that leant down to grasp the sea was solidifying and putting on flesh.

'There's nothing we can do,' I said.

We had no awnings up and the sails were stowed. There was no time to try and get out to sea. We could only watch and wait. If the spout hit the boat, and the anchor dragged, *Mother Goose* might fetch up on the beach.

'I'll start the engine—just in case.'

The wind's note changed suddenly. We could see the spray rising thirty or forty feet high where the grey trunk drank the water. It was so close now, swirling and curving round the end of the point, that we could hear a hard hiss like a giant kettle boiling, and we both jumped into the cockpit.

'I'll take the tiller,' I said. 'You stand by the throttle. We'll ease the strain on the cable.'

Mother Goose was sidling and twisting, first to port then to starboard, as conflicting eddies whirled about us. I kicked over the gear lever and we began to forge slowly ahead.

'Enough!'

We stopped and drifted back a little on the cable. The spout was right off the end of the mole now, a hundred yards from where we lay. The wind tugged at the boat. There was a moaning noise and the edge of the dark cloud came right over us. My palms were sweating and Janet's face was drawn. A burst of rain rattled like shrapnel on the coach-roof.

'It's——'

The dark twister was howling and the base of the trunk leaned sideways. Then it moved quick and sudden, with a curious flexible shudder, and spun away across the harbour—going away from us.

The wind was whipping round the boat like the leaves of a thousand autumns. A back eddy caught us on the starboard quarter, spinning us right round, and I could feel that bumping, slithering movement as we began to drag. Janet slapped over the gear lever and raised the throttle as I tried to head into the wind. Then another side-current caught us on the bow and knocked us off to port. The spout was going through the harbour like a motor boat out of control, twisting and skimming. There was a shouting crowd on the deck of the fishing boat. I had no time to see what they were doing—either letting out more cable or trying to get under way.

'We're dragging!'

Our stern was right round to the jetty now and we were coming down fast on it. Under full power we just managed to ease away and get some sea under our tail. The anchor had clearly broken out from the bottom and had had no chance to sink its teeth again.

'Look at that!' Janet pointed.

The base of the waterspout was hovering just on the edge of the shore, close to the rowing boats. Sand and water, dust and pebbles were whirling up into the air, and an awning took to the sky, flapping away like a great grey ghost. We could watch it calmly now. It was well past us and there was no more danger to the boat. Out in the middle of the harbour we eased the engine and rested. The grey arm had changed its colour and was tawny from sand and muddy earth. It had a mad, angry quality as if losing the sea had changed its nature. One of the rowing boats was knocked over on its side and men were tearing about like ants disturbed from under a stone.

'Antonio's boat,' said Janet.

'He'd have done better to stay with us.'

The waterspout was climbing the hill towards the castle. Branches of trees, leaves, and driftwood were whipped into the air. The roof of someone's shack soared up. It hovered, hung for a second, and then began to slip-slop back to the ground, idling from side to side like a falling leaf.

The spout was breaking up. It seemed as if the weight of the roof had proved too much for it to carry, for halfway up the hill the *tromba* gave a last flick and a shudder. It bent backwards from the middle and collapsed in a heavy thunder of water. It sounded as if a dam had burst, and the water fell with a great solid slap! a few yards short of a row of cottages.

'*Mamma mia!*' I said.

'*Tromba marina!*' said Janet. 'That's one nautical word I reckon we won't forget in a hurry.'

No one was killed, no one hurt even. The total damage reported to us by Antonio was five chickens lost, and a dog—not his—with a broken leg. His own boat had fallen on its side when he and his sons had jumped out to try and save their neighbour's awning.

'But there will be more today,' he said. 'This time of year sometimes there are many. It is a long time, though, since one of them crossed the harbour.'

We anchored again well out from the shore, quite near to the harbour entrance. If any of them came our way I was going to get out and have sea room in which to manœuvre.

'Do you remember that yacht hand last year?' said Janet. We were taking a strong drink in the comforting warmth of the cabin. 'I really believe him now.'

He was an Italian yacht hand whom we had met on the west coast of Italy. He had been sailing an old 30-square-metre down to meet his owner in Naples, and he had told us how a few weeks before, single-handed off Elba, he had nearly been wrecked by a waterspout.

'Yes, I remember him,' I said. 'I knew I'd heard the words *Tromba marina* before.'

He told us how he had taken down all his sails and was under engine, passing through the centre of a thunder-storm. It was midnight and very dark except for the lightning flashes. 'Suddenly,' he said, 'there was a terrible roaring and the boat spun round. I could not hold the tiller and the noise was so great, signore, that I could not even tell whether the engine was still running. The boat heeled over so far I thought she would sink.'

'What did you do?' we asked.

'I took a quick turn with the tiller lines to keep the tiller central—then I ran below and closed the hatch after me.'

'And . . . ?'

'Ah, I prayed, signore. How I prayed! I prayed to the Holy Virgin and to Her Son and to all the Saints to save me.'

After five minutes, when the boat had come back on an even keel, he had put his head out and surveyed the damage. Everything movable had disappeared from the upper deck—ropes, sails, oars, and even the dinghy. Only the mast was still standing.

'I thought at the time it was a bit of an old salt's yarn,' I said. 'I remember thinking how typical he could do nothing better than pray. I understand him now. If you ran into one of those at night it wouldn't leave you must option except get down on your knees.'

Janet raised her glass. 'Cheers—let's hope we won't have to.'

We counted six other waterspouts that day, but we were lucky and all of them passed well to seaward. We sat watching them through the binoculars, tense, and ready to jump to it if any of them had shown a shift towards the anchorage. It was one of those days when you wish that there were more of you in the boat: when the strain of keeping an anchor watch and of being—between the two of you—captain, navigator, cook, engineer, electrician, plumber, shipwright, and crew makes you frayed and irritable.

'I'm flogged,' I said. 'I hope to God this weather doesn't hold. Perhaps we'd do better to get out and go up to Riposto or back to Augusta—into a real harbour. I'm fed up with this.'

Janet took the bad days with more resilience than I did.

'I don't see any point in moving,' she said. 'In a crowded harbour we'd have less anchor room—other boats dragging down on us, cables all over the place. You know what it's like. Besides, this weather isn't going to last.'

She was right, and in the late afternoon a pale sunlight flickered through. The horizon cleared to a watery blue and the dark clouds went away, on into the hills and over the island. The washing began to come out in the streets and to flutter from the house windows. The fishermen pulled their boats down the beach and youths were diving from the breakwater and swimming out towards us. The commandante rowed up and showed us a weather report: a depression was moving over Sicily from the north-east. The cold front would follow in twelve to twenty-four hours, but in two or three days the settled weather would return.

'It is often like this in September,' he said. 'Just a week or so, then it will be fine again. You will see.'

We stayed in Porto Brucoli three days and it was good to be tucked away, even if it was only a semi-sheltered harbour. We could hear the wind over the headland and there was a short sharp sea outside. The autumn had come with a coolness at nights and a scent of rain-washed earth. Sometimes we could smell wood-smoke, and sometimes the smell of pitch from a fishing boat that was being tarred and caulked on the foreshore.

SIXTEEN

I WORKED on my book during the days, and Janet busied herself with the boat. In the evenings we rowed ashore and went to the harbour-master's office to see the weather bulletin. Often he had a friend with him, a cheerful round-faced man in his forties who ran the village store. He had been in the army during the war and had been captured in the Western Desert. His English was good, for he had spent three years as a prisoner near Norwich, and if Janet was not with me he would tell me of his successes with the Norfolk girls.

'If I had not been married,' he said, 'I would have stayed there. I have a small son in England. Yes, I would like to have stayed there and maybe one day bought my own land.'

He told the harbour-master how much it had rained, and how the wind came off the North Sea as cold as the snow on Etna. 'But the soil,' he said, 'it is so rich, and the wheat is better even than on the plains of Catania.'

Sometimes Janet and I would walk down the village street which straggled back towards the old castle. We would sit in one of the dark bars where the ceiling was hung with salami, garlic, and dried cod, and drink some of the rough wine. Then we would climb to the castle where the ramparts fell sheer away and look out over the sea. We would watch the lights of cars crossing the Catania plain and the twinkle of the city in the distance. At night there were a few of the bigger fishing boats working off the coast, so we knew that we could easily move on if we wanted to—but it was good to spend a few days in this village. I was able to work undisturbed, and Janet was going over the clothes we should need for the winter—old tweeds, jerseys, serge trousers, shirts, and socks. They had been stowed away in a kitbag since the end of March.

We were sitting one night in the small trattoria where the harbour-master sometimes went for his meals when a gaunt grey-haired man came over. It was the end of the week and, like many of the locals, he was clearly a Wednesday and Sunday shaver. His face was drowned in grey stubble, and his hair stuck out round his head as though he had just got out of bed.

'Good evening—you permit me?' His English creaked, as if it was a door in an old house that had not been opened for many years. The old woman who ran the place came up with a chair. She was full of deference.

'The Barone B——' he introduced himself.

He had seen our boat in the harbour. It was a long time since he had last met any English people, not since before the war when he and his father had been in the habit of visiting Malta once a year.

'Malta is much the same,' I said, 'a little knocked about since those days.'

The barone sipped his wine and explained his mission.

'I am a pipe-smoker and good pipes are unobtainable in Porto Brucoli nowadays.'

He wondered if, by any chance, I as an Englishman—who naturally smoked a pipe—had one to spare, or one that I could trade with him.

'I have several,' I said.

I had bought them from the pipe factory in Malta and they were made of good Calabrian briar. I knew there were two or three unsmoked and I would be only too happy to make him a present. One of the hens, which were always scuttling in and out of the place, ran across the room and the woman gave it a sharp kick—as if to say, 'Not when the barone is present!'

He came down to the shore with us, whistling up one of the villagers whom we passed and giving him some message. There were many barones in Sicily and southern Italy. The title was rather like that of 'squire'. It meant little more than that he was the chief landowner in the village. I do not think the Barone B.'s estates were large. He was a wry figure in his dusty black coat and sponge-bag trousers. His English improved after a drink, and I found the pipes and asked him to take whichever he pleased. He took a short-stemmed briar with a big bowl, thanking me with many turns of old-fashioned courtesy. I regretted I had no tobacco I could spare. I did not mind Italian cigarettes, but their pipe tobacco was hot and dusty. I had stocked up with English tobacco in Malta before we left, but I had hardly enough to see me through the coming months.

When we rowed back the man whom he had spoken to was waiting on the shore. He had a sack on his shoulder and he put it down to assist the barone to land.

'It is a small return,' said the barone, 'a small-enough return for your magnificent present. Your wife will find that they cook well.' He handed me the sack which was heavy and rustled crisply with small golden onions,

'The finest onions in Sicily,' he said.

It was now my turn to say that this was more, far more, than the small gift of the pipe warranted. Janet was very pleased with the onions. They were those small, firm-fleshed ones that go well with pasta, or in fish soup or a ragout, and for many weeks afterwards we blessed the barone once a day.

Our fourth night in Porto Brucoli was calm, with a soft sky and all the stars. We said goodbye and stood farewell drinks to the harbour-master and his friend, to Antonio and the others. We would be leaving in the morning. All the fishermen were going out that night and we watched them pull out round the point and work their way seaward. Their lights went on up the coast, like a string of pearls unfolding.

We had set the alarm for half past four, so as to get under way with the dawn. But it was only four o'clock when I heard a boat come alongside. In it was Antonio and his sons.

'*Scusi, signore.* We hoped not to disturb you. I have put a few fish on the side there for you and the lady. They are some of the first we have caught since this bad weather started. We thought you would both like something fresh for your meal tomorrow—when you are out at sea.'

Their smiles were vivid in the hissing lamp-light. There was a lot of water in their small boat, and their clothes were stained with salt and heavy with spray.

'How is it out there?' I asked. 'You look wet. And the fish, Antonio —I would like to give you something for them.'

'It is quite rough,' he said. 'Only the swell left over, though. There is no wind. For the fish—nothing. Please, nothing.'

Janet came out and they greeted her.

'It's just like Levanzo,' I said to her. 'They've brought us fish and they won't take anything for them.'

'They look cold and tired,' she said. 'I'll get them some brandy.'

'And cigarettes,' I said.

She came back with the bottle and glasses and a tin of cigarettes. I poured them half a tumblerful each and handed the drinks down into the boat. Antonio raised his glass.

'Your health and the lady's. Come back to Brucoli again.'

After the boat had pulled away I put on the cockpit light and looked at the fish. They were small sole; delicate, and speckled with pink and blue dots. Antonio had wrapped them in seaweed to keep them fresh, and they still trembled under their dark-green covering. They brought with them a memory of the world they had just left—the surge of the swell as it lifted over the banks, and the rasp of sand along their flat bellies. They smelled of the salt night and the moving sea.

SEVENTEEN

THE sea has two faces, and so has the island. If there are *gregales* at sea, there is poverty inland. If there are water-spouts and thunder-storms to hazard the fishermen, there is the mafia and the legacy of centuries of oppression to harass the peasant.

'. . . Your letters,' a friend wrote, 'describe a world that I had forgotten existed. But how about the ignorance and the poverty and the lack of sanitation?'

But the life of the land is different from the life at sea and on the coast. Fishermen and sailors, and those who make their living by the sea, are not the same as men who work the land. Their horizons are wider and their life brings them into contact with other people and places. The white sun of summer which burns the inland mountains and dries the pastures to powder is different for the man on the deck of a fishing boat. The sea around the island is over-fished, but a man can still get a living, and from the level of our own small boat, on a budget of about four pounds a week—much the same as many a local fisherman—we were not presented with any varnished or deceptive portrait.

The deep-etched squalor of the mountain villages, the harsh life of the land, and the sun-dried earth washing into the gullies with the autumn rains (because the trees have gone)—these were not part of our world. People who live on, or by, the sea always have the sight and sound of it to make up for poverty and squalor. As the old man said who took our lines in Messina: 'I have no work for nearly two months. But the day is good and the sea is beautiful. This afternoon I go and fish from the breakwater.'

I gave him some lire and a cup of coffee. This evening he would come back and sleep on our foredeck. Messina is a bad place for thieves, for in Messina the modern world of industry and commerce meets the ancient world of traditional beliefs and a decaying feudal system. The two do not make good bedfellows. And then, the memory of too many disasters hangs over Messina. Its position dominating the Straits between Sicily and the mainland has made it one of the most fought-over places on earth: almost every invasion or occupation of the island has begun or ended here. Corruption and disaster are in the air, and it is not only the memory of the great earthquake which gives the city its ready-to-be-abandoned feeling. It was here that the great plague started in Europe.

'I just saw a rat on the jetty,' said Janet as we were having lunch.

'We'd better try and keep them off the boat.'

The great plague was rat-borne. It was in October 1347 that some Venetian galleys sailed into this half-moon harbour and brought with them from the East the rats—and the fleas on the rats—which introduced the plague into Europe. The pestilence was unequalled even in the past, and up to now has never been approached. It had started in China in 1334, and it ravaged the world for close on thirty years. During that time sixty million people died—about a third of the population of the world. No pandemic in history has remotely compared with the great plague, and its after-effects were long-lasting and profound. Age-old conceptions of the position of the individual, the family, Church and State were shaken. With it died the Middle Ages, and it was here in dusty Messina that the germ—not only of plague but of so many other things—first reached Europe.

We had come up to the city under a fair wind, with slack water in the Straits. We had seen no signs or marvels and I for one was inclined to believe that Ulysses was something of a yarn-spinner in his old age. 'Lamenting, we sailed up the narrow strait. For on one side lay Scylla and on the other immortal Charybdis swallowed down the salt sea-water in a terrifying way. When she belched it forth it was like a cauldron on a hot fire as she bubbled and seethed. High overhead the spray fell on the tops of both the headlands. When she sucked down the sea she was in utter turmoil, and the rock nearby roared terrifyingly. Beneath her the sea bed could be seen, dark with sand.'

'Through the Straits tomorrow,' said Janet.

'Well, we had no trouble last year, coming down.'

'Only a few tide-rips.'

'We'll go up with the *Montante*,' I said. 'That should make it easy.'

The main current in the Straits runs from north to south for a period of six hours, then there is a stand of the tide until it sets in again in the opposite direction. The north-going current is known as the *Montante* and the south-going the *Scendente*. It is strong at spring tides, sometimes making as much as four and a half knots. Last year we had come through at neaps, but it was just about springs now. Still, I was not worried. I had come through the Straits many times during the war and never seen a thing. Of course, in a destroyer with all that power under your belt, you sometimes got a false impression of the sea.

'What do you think about the current in the Straits?' I asked the old man when he came back in the evening.

'Quite fierce now, signore. My cousin has been out fishing today. He says it is strong enough.'

I had been watching the fishing boats that afternoon, dozens of them scudding backwards and forwards between Sicily and the mainland. The narrow blue stretch had been skimming with their sails, like the wings of gulls. It had been a fine afternoon and the peaks of the Peloritan mountains behind the city had been sharp and clear.

'It will blow from the north tomorrow,' he said. 'Sometimes when the wind is from the north there is a brutal sea in the Straits.'

A north wind meant that we should have to go through under power as well as sail. The wind would siphon hard through the narrow mouth. It was blowing from the north already and that was why the mountains were so distinct.

'I want to get some *vino*,' I said. 'Can you show me a good place?'

He put down the clothes and the blanket that he was carrying and scratched his head.

'Give them to me,' I said. 'My wife is aboard. She will look after them until we come back. I'll put an awning over the deck here for you to sleep under.'

'There's no need for that, signore. There will be no dampness with this wind. Not like the sirocco.'

We walked across the Corso Vittorio Emmanuale (I expect they had changed its name, but the old man like everyone else still used the old one) and down one of the side streets. In five minutes we were into the shanty town of the poor; the temporary buildings designed to fall swiftly with the next earthquake. Hens and children dived in front of us and scraps of paper twirled in the breeze. There was vitality, though, and cheerfulness. Several times we were greeted.

'Relatives,' he explained. He certainly seemed to have a lot of nephews and nieces, for each one called him 'uncle'. The bar belonged to his cousin, the same one who had been out fishing that afternoon. He was tall and lean, with red eyes strained from staring into the sun's track on the water. I brought out the empty bottles from the string bag I was carrying and stacked them on the bar.

'The signore wants some wine,' said the old man.

'White or black? You don't mind? Try a little glass of each first then. The black is good.'

They call the red wine *nero*, or black, in Sicily. Most of the local wine is strong and sharp and a good deal of it is shipped up to northern Italy to give body to the weaker Chiantis. Some of the stuff I had drunk along the south coast would take the enamel off your teeth and leave it on the roof of your mouth, but this wine in Messina was not too bad.

'Please fill the three bottles with the black,' I said, 'and the one big bottle with white. The white pleases my wife more.'

'It is a little more sweet,' said the landlord. 'Better for the ladies.'

We had some black olives and a few thin shavings of mortadella with our drinks. Just as we were leaving, the landlord hauled out a large dark bottle from behind the bar.

'Vecchio Alkamak,' he said. 'Try it, signore. The best wine in Sicily.'

The bottle was rare in that part of the world for having a brand name on it, as well as a picture of a contented-looking family sipping their wine over a meal. Some export stuff, I thought, probably like Marsala. Not for me, but I'll have a glass so as not to offend.

'Good?' he asked as I tasted it.

He was right. It was the best wine I had had in Sicily; full and round, with a bouquet; something like a madeira, and with none of that sweetness which spoils most Sicilian export wines. It had the colour of a tawny port, and all the ripeness of autumn.

'Magnificent!' I said. 'That's something!'

It was more than double the price of the ordinary wine from the cask but I took three two-litre bottles with me. It would be just the drink after supper, on an evening when the air had the tang of rain and the mists were gathering in the folds below the hills.

When we got back to the boat I rigged an awning over the foredeck. The old man had some bread and soup with us, and I gave him the riding light to take forward with him.

'Would you like the *Giornale?*' I asked. I had bought it that morning. The Four Powers were talking about meeting somewhere or other some day when they could get around to it. The Pope had had a vision. There had been a kidnapping on the road leading into Palermo from Montelepre.

'*Grazie, signore.*' He looked at the picture on the front page.

'*Il Papa,*' he said.

I knew by the way he handled the paper that he could not read. There were many who could not read in Sicily, but they were little the worse for that. Men who could not read—as I had often found—were quicker on the uptake than those who could. If you explained something to a man who could not read, he remembered it and it needed no second explanation. A mechanic in Sciacca, back in the spring, had done a decoke on the diesel engine with me. He had never seen that type of engine before, but he had shown an acuteness which was often lacking in the man who had to keep consulting a grubby manual.

'Of making many books there is no end; and much study is a weariness of the flesh.' But, in the meantime, 'The sleep of a labouring man is sweet, whether he eat little or much . . .' and in the night when I got up, hearing the wind in the rigging, the old man was asleep. He woke, though, the minute I put my foot on the coach-roof, and raised himself on his elbow.

'What is it, Captain?' he asked.

'Nothing,' I said. 'I heard the wind, that's all. You are not cold?'

'No, it is not cold in this month. Have no fear for robbers. No one will trouble the little boat.'

The moon was full and the sky was very clear.

'Go to sleep, Captain. I will wake you in the morning.'

EIGHTEEN

THE day broke cold. The Straits were shining, and the land over by Reggio on the Italian side seemed only a few yards away. We stood on deck and watched one of the ferry boats come in. Her decks were crowded with passengers and we saw how she sidled into the harbour, her bows pointing a little south of the entrance, yet the current bearing her north.

'It's certainly running,' said Janet.

'Well, we'll give it a try. Time's getting on.'

We aimed to go up to the Lipari islands about fifty miles north and sail through them on our way to the west coast of Sicily. We were due in Palermo by the end of October.

The old man gave us a hand to cast off our lines.

'Come back if it is too strong!' he called. 'This wind will not last. By tomorrow the passage will be easier.'

An open fishing boat came bucketing in as we cleared the breakwater and ran up our sails. We would head out for about a quarter of a mile, and then tack back towards the coast again. I knew from last year that it was best to keep close inshore when going through the narrow part and then hug the land near Cape Peloro. There was a light on the cape marking the north-eastern point of Sicily. We would have to watch out for the shoal just off the point.

The wind was gusty outside the harbour and there were tide-rips spreading across the Straits to the north as we ran out quickly, passing one or two fishing boats. We made no leeway, for the current pushed us steadily northward, and when we turned and came about, Messina was behind us.

'It's a sailing day all right,' I said.

'Yes.' Janet looked up at the mainsail. 'If it doesn't get too strong. It might have been wise to take a reef before we came out.'

'Too late to worry now. If it gets that strong we'll just have to drop the main and try it under engine and staysail.'

The spray was sparky and the rushing crystal of a wave came up under our stern. A few drops fell into the cockpit. The sea was veined with green and white.

'I'll just check that everything's good and secure below,' said Janet. 'We don't want any repetition of the disaster off Porto Bruccoli.' (In the end we had had to take up the whole carpet and boil it in a cauldron on the foreshore to get out the tomato paste.)

'Okay,' I said. 'You'll know when we get into the overfalls!'

Even without the glasses I could see that there was a line of white across the Straits, about quarter of a mile away. Where the two shores narrowed on each other, the north-going current was meeting the swell driven down against it by the wind. It was going to be bumpy.

'You'd better shut the skylight,' I called down. 'We don't want the Captain to get soaked.'

We were running in now towards the coast and I noticed that the Straits were rather deserted. There was a steamer going away up north and the ferry had just crossed to Reggio. All the small boats seemed to have disappeared. But when I looked astern I was comforted to see that there were still a number of them about. This morning they were keeping a long way down, though, for it would be no good fishing where the water was too broken.

The sea-swirl was only a hundred yards or so away now. I could hear the sound of the breaking water quite distinctly—countless small explosions of turning waves and bursting spray.

Slap! We were into it, and the first toppling sea broke clean over the bows. I let the boat fall off a little to port, taking the wind more on the beam so as to make better speed.

Janet came out and joined me.

'The sooner we're through this, the better.'

Mother Goose began to buck and dance. The sea was confused, coming at us from every side, and a broken crest jumped the weather rail and burst in the cockpit. The drainaways gurgled and we were standing in a foot of water as another crest came over. The wind gave an angry flap in the mainsail and I saw that it was beginning to head us. We would either have to drop the main and close the shore under power, or tack out again.

'Ready about!'

We ducked our heads as the boom swung over. There was an angry crackle and a thundering from the bows. One of the jib sheets had fouled up and Janet scrambled forward to clear it.

'Let's stand out once more,' I said as she crawled back into the cockpit. 'If it's too strong in the middle we'll have to come about again. Then next time—as soon as the wind begins to head us—we'll have to drop the main.'

Long before we had got into the centre of the Straits it was clear that the full mainsail was too much for her in this wind. We began to heel and put our lee scupper under—and when a Dutch boat's scuppers are awash she is over-canvased. We came about again and the wind was really fierce now. It came with a shout and the spray was blinding, the water dripped from our hair into our eyes and ran in cold cascades inside our shirts. The boat was hardly manageable in the confusion of breaking waves. She staggered and yawed, and the long tiller was thrown about under my arm, so that I had to brace my feet hard against the sides of the cockpit-combing to keep my balance. The mainsail began to snarl and flap as we closed the coast.

'Bloody wind's coming off the land again,' I said. 'Can you take her?'

We stood there together for a few seconds until Janet got the feel of her, then I clambered forward to the foot of the mast. The deck was jumping as I grabbed the halyards and let the mainsail down with a run. There was only time to put one tie round the belly of it. I tumbled back into the cockpit and put up the throttle to full power.

'Okay?'

Janet nodded. We kept the bows pointed in towards the shore and gradually the broken sea and the shift of tumbling water drew astern of us. We were under the lee of the land now and the going was easier every minute.

'That wasn't too pleasant.'

The sun was warm on our backs and our clothes began to steam. We were coming up level with Cape Peloro, close in under the land, nearing the narrowest neck of the Straits.

'More broken water ahead,' she said.

There was a curious swirl on the surface a few cables away. It didn't look like the overfalls which we had just left behind. There was a smooth glassy quality about it—and yet the water was moving.

'It's a whirlpool!' I said.

I could see now that there was a distinct dip in the middle of it, and the small white waves were all moving round and round. Janet swung the tiller hard over. We altered course away towards the centre of the Straits. We were about four hundred yards off the lighthouse and the circling water was moving quite slowly like a gyro-top losing its impetus. Or was it only just beginning to spin? The heart of it was just abeam of us, about a hundred yards away. There was froth on the surface all round the boat, but the moving centre had a treacly consistency, like boiled sugar when it is cooling off.

As we left it behind the wind opened up and put its weight into the stay-sail. I relieved Janet at the tiller while she got the *Sicily Pilot* out of the locker.

'Charybdis, all right,' she said. 'Two or three hundred yards offshore abreast the tower.'

'That's the lady.'

' "There is every reason to suppose," ' she read, ' "that Charybdis was rather more impressive then—in classical times—than it is today." '

'Ulysses was telling the truth after all. I take back anything I may have said. Even the way it is now would be pretty grim. And it was hardly spinning.'

Janet put the glasses on it.

'It's moving faster,' she said. 'Am I glad we've dropped it astern. It must have been just starting when we passed it. Not that it would have sunk us, but I'm wet enough already.'

Over on the Italian side, where Scylla had once laid another trap for the unwary, there was nothing stirring. A few broken eddies near the rock, that was all, and the old town looked peaceful under the sun. We came in close by the beach where the waves swirled up the pale sand and the fishing boats were drawn back out of harm's way. There were nets spread to dry along the shore and the smoke from the chimneys was sliding fast to the south. We took a deep reef in the main and then rehoisted it as we set course towards the Liparis.

It was good to be out of those narrow waters and I had learned a new respect for Homeric accuracy. Before 1783, when a violent earthquake changed the sea-bed, all the reports seem to show that Scylla and Charybdis were very real dangers to small boats. To the ancient Greek sailors, who had never come across tides before, the narrow Straits of Messina must have been terrible and haunted. Beneath all the myth-spinning and the legendary nature of the Odyssey there was a deep sub-stratum of accurate reportage. What were the rocks that the one-eyed Cyclops had hurled at the mariners but stones tossed from Etna during an eruption? There were a lot of other things that became clearer when you sailed this sea as we were doing. Dawn really was 'rosy-fingered', especially if there were clouds about, or if there was water vapour in the air, the way you got it with a sirocco.

'You'll get drowned one day,' said Janet. 'Daydreaming at the tiller. That's the way Shelley went.'

'Yes, but you know what Trelawny said—"Shelley had never had his hands in a tar bucket and needed a haircut". And only a poet would have dreamed of sailing through a Mediterranean thunder-storm with a gaff topsail set over an open boat.'

'Don't be too smug,' she said, 'and watch out for those squalls.'

The wind was still in the north, but squalls were beginning to fan off the Calabrian mountains across the open sea. The boat was going well with the wind almost on the beam and we were steering north-west towards the centre of the Lipari islands. From the end of the Straits we had about forty miles to go and at our present speed we ought to reach them sometime that evening.

'There's one that's travelling!' Janet said.

A lateen-rigged fishing boat was cutting across our bows, bound out of the Gulf of Gioja and heading down towards Sicily. She was a real Homeric boat, about forty foot long, and all the old epithets applied to her. She was 'swift'—making some six or seven knots—and 'well balanced'; that you could tell by the way she lifted to the swell and soared over the crests. She was 'hollow', too—an open boat, that's to say—and she was 'black'. Her sides glistened and it was plain she had just been freshly tarred. On the leeside one man was rowing to stop her from crabbing downwind.

She went by with a lift and a swagger some twenty yards away. The helmsman was standing up balancing the tiller between his thighs, the oarsman was working away in a slow steady rhythm, and two others were busy amidships hauling down on the tackle at the foot of the sail. A fine rain of spray drifted over them all the time and there was a rainbow over the bows. She looked as if she had sailed off a Greek vase.

'One of the swordfish boats,' I said.

Along that part of the northern coast of Sicily, between Messina and Milazzo, there was good fishing at the season when the swordfish closed the coast to spawn. The fishing was a traditional industry round there and families had the sections of sea opposite their part of the beach assigned to them. Poaching on a neighbour's water had led to many a feud. When the big fish were in along the coast the boats went out with a man standing aloft on a small crow's-nest. He was the master of the fishing, for only he could see the gliding shapes of the swordfish way ahead of the boat's bows. The harpoonist often fired blind—a hand-thrown harpoon—acting entirely on the orders of the man aloft. 'Sweet as a grape,' the old man in Messina had described the swordfish. It was rich-fleshed and the best eating in that part of the world, better even than tunny. I had been tunny fishing off Sciacca and Favignana, but next year I hoped to go out in a Swordfish boat.

In the late afternoon we watched the sun go down behind the hump-back of Vulcano, the southernmost of the Lipari islands.

'I wonder why they were called the Isles of Aeolus?' I said. 'I mean, I wonder why they believed the God of the Winds lived here especially?'

As we neared the straits between Vulcano and Lipari the winds began to pipe around us. They were typical island squalls like those we had met in Greece, and they whipped over the dark sea with sudden anger. Squalls at night were frightening. You could not see them coming and only the sudden rise in the wind's note gave you any warning of their approach. Reluctantly we had to lower sails and motor into a rising sea.

'Look!' said Janet.

There was a glow on the horizon, like the lights of a distant city—but this was pulsating.

'Stromboli.'

The volcano was always active, but recently it had been erupting violently and we had been warned in Messina not to sail too close to it at any time, for rocks, pumice, and ash were being hurled into the sea around. A thin ribbon of fire fluttered and glowed down one side.

In the wild night, with the sudden bursts of wind and the loom of the islands against the sky and the fires of Stromboli ahead, we had a swift understanding of why they were called the Isles of Aeolus. People in steamships might dismiss the hazards of Scylla and Charybdis, of Strom-boli and of Aeolus, as poetic fancy. We knew better. Even with our modern charts, our compass, and our diesel engine we found them memorable.

We were nearing the harbour of Lipari and I was shining the torch on to the chart when suddenly—slap!—something struck me hard on the cheek. There was a rustle and a brittle fluttering around my feet. I looked down.

'Hey!'

'What's up?' Janet called from the bows.

A flying fish, attracted by the light, had leaped over the gunwale. If it hadn't struck my face it would probably have gone on clean over the boat.

Hardly a second later there was a flop! and another flutter. A second one fell into the scuppers. *Angeletti* ('little angels'), the fishermen call them. You can see why in daytime, when they rise from the sea in their bright silver showers.

Janet laughed as I rubbed my cheek. 'It wasn't the light that brought them in. It was that great moon-face.'

The flying fish were about half a pound in weight, graceless now, and good only for one thing.

'Breakfast,' I said.

A last squall whipped overhead with a dry rustle like paper twirling down an autumn street. The lights on the breakwater were quite close. We were very tired.

NINETEEN

THERE was no cloud, no wind, and the sea was calm. The sun had set over an hour ago and we were motoring south into the Gulf of Castellammare. It was over a week since we had left Messina and since then we had been cruising through the Liparis.

They were strange islands, with their contrast of arid volcanic peaks and green richness where the terraced slopes of vines climbed the mountains. I had a lump of glassy black obsidian from Lipari to remind me of them, and *Mother Goose* had lost her waterline weed by lying off a beach where a sulphur stream came to the surface. From Alicudi, the westernmost island, we had crossed to Ustica, the lone rocky peak that lies off the north-west coast of Sicily. Now we knew not only the coastline, but all the rugged outriders of Sicily; from Gozo and Malta in the south, to Marettimo in the west, and Stromboli in the far north. The Liparis were the harshest and wildest of all. Mussolini, like the Roman emperors, had used them as a place of banishment for political prisoners, and on Ustica, too, there was a prison. The islands still wore the desiccating air of exile —something that was only just redeemed by the sight of fishing boats leaning across from island to island, or the green flanks of Monte Salvatore with the clouds swelling around the peak.

We had left Ustica early that morning and we had been over twelve hours at sea when we raised the coast of Sicily. There were many lights along the coast and we were glad to be coming back.

'We're nearly there,' I said.

Janet was standing on the foredeck with the glasses.

'I can see them!' she called. 'Come to port a little. I can see the rocks. They're dead ahead.'

I eased the engine and stood up on the seat to get a better view. I could just make out the shine of them about quarter of a mile away. We were aiming to drop anchor in the small cove of Torre Scopello, in the lee of two tall rocks, I Faraglioni, that lie at the head of the Gulf. There were a few houses there and the buildings of a tunny fishery, but the nets had been taken in long ago. The fishing was over by the end of summer, and all the tunny caught that year would have been canned by now.

'We can come right in close,' I said. 'It's deep water all the way.'

We dropped anchor a few yards off the beach in six fathoms, with a bottom of sand and weed. It was a still night and no lights gleamed from the buildings on the foreshore. A car passed well inland, on the road to Castellammare, its head-lamps bouncing and dipping, catching the silver sides of a hill. We had eaten our stew a few hours before and we did not even stop for a drink or a cup of tea before crawling into our bunks.

When I woke it was just after six o'clock; I could see the brass-rimmed clock on the bulkhead and beneath it the barometer. On either side, the glass-fronted bookshelves with their bright colours were shining in the early light. The deckhead above me reflected the shift and ripple of water. We had left the hatch open and, though the cabin was warm, it was full of the fresh morning air.

Janet was asleep and the Captain's head was turned back into the feathers under his wing. The chart was still spread out on the table, held down by the parallel ruler, the pencil box, and my old brass dividers. A small pencil cross marked the place where we were anchored. Behind it the line of our course zigzagged back to Ustica, across to the Liparis and then down to Messina. I liked to leave our fixes and position lines on the chart until we had moved on to the next one. Then, on a leisured evening, we could check them against the log before rubbing them out. There was no value, perhaps, in such accuracy but I liked to feel that once I had sailed these seas I would preserve a permanent record of them, as well as the sights, scents, and sounds that my memory had stored away.

'*L'automne déjà!—Mais pourquoi regretter un éternel soleil, si nous sommes engagés à la découverture de la clarté divin,—loins des gens qui meurent sur les saisons.*' I looked at the book open on the table. Rimbaud had never come to Sicily, but he would no more have found what he was looking for here than in Abyssinia. Like all perfectionists it was the unattainable island for which he was navigating.

The carpet was cool under my feet. It had absorbed some of the dampness of the night air. I opened the galley door quietly, took down the bottle of methylated spirit from the shelf and primed th ecup under the burner. When the flame began to flicker and die I turned on the tap from the paraffin tank and waited to hear the plop and hiss as the vapour caught fire. It would take about five minutes for the kettle to boil.

The deck of the cockpit was stained with dew. The furled mainsail was beaded, and a spider's web trembled between the boom and the coach-roof. The wimpel at the masthead hung vertical in the windless air. A hardly perceptible swell was sending round the edge of the rocks, just enough to make the boat lift gently and soundlessly every now and again.

It would be a fine day. Out to sea the horizon was faint with mist, and a small coaster under power was moving eastwards towards Palermo. There were no rowing boats or fishing boats in sight; the night-fishermen would have returned with the dawn, and the day-fishermen would not be out for an hour or so. There were several fishing villages in this gulf, and we would see their boats scattered over the bay long before noon.

I got a soft rag from one of the cockpit lockers and began to wipe the seats and the varnished woodwork. The brown surface had a bloom on it from the damp, and in places the varnish was already beginning to crack and peel away as fine as rice paper. We were lying with our stern towards the beach and I looked to see if anyone was stirring. There was a solitary rowing boat drawn high up by one of the buildings, but that was all. Three of the buildings looked deserted; they were storage sheds for the tunny fishery most probably. In front of one of them was stacked row upon row of the great anchors with which they moored the tunny nets. At the head of the small beach there was an arch like a bridge under one of the cottages—one of the winter torrents must come out just there from the hill behind. To the right of the beach the innermost of I Faraglioni took the sun, a romantic silver rock with shrubs and thyme and wild grasses clinging to its sides. After the long heats of summer the land behind was quite bare, except where a few scattered olives broke the soil.

I made myself a cup of tea and went back and sat out in the cockpit. Clouds were beginning to form over the island and I sat and watched the birth of a fair-weather cumulus.

A light haze began to lift out of a valley and, as it drifted, a mist which had been hanging over the nearby hillside slid towards it. An unseen dip in the hill discharged, like a minute gun, a small puff of smoke. The land was beginning to warm, and soon every bank and fold and cave was firing white shells into the air. The cloud thickened and darkened. The wind blew it sideways and, as it rose, it toppled into the shape of an old man's head. After half an hour it was full-grown, and it drifted inland to join the other morning clouds.

I got my bathing trunks out of the after locker, and slung the rope ladder over the side. A flurry of small fish darted away at the splash. The water was quite warm, but nowadays there was just a faint shock on getting into it. I swam inshore towards the rocks and browsed along the fringe of them. Later in the day I would come fishing here with the spear-gun. There would be rockfish in the crannies, and there might even be flatfish of some kind out among the sand of the bay. There would almost certainly be octopus among the rocks. Now that we had got the hang of skinning them we took them whenever we could, for the diced tentacles had a good flavour—even if they were always a bit tough.

I landed and walked along the cool beach. There were small wave-runs in the sand, but the rowing boat had clearly been dragged up the beach some time ago. The scraped line that her keel must have made had disappeared, and there had been no wind in the night to scatter the effacing sand. Sticks, stones, and a few sea-shells—the usual debris of a beach. I came on an empty tin, with its lid hinged back, that had probably been used as a bailer in the boat; a fragment of an old inner tube; and a strand of silk that had once been dark but was now faded from salt and sun. I picked it up. Just visible, the metallic thread almost rotted away, were the letters 'H.M.S.' An old naval cap tally!

It lay among a drift of sea-wreck in a scoop of sand where some wave higher than the rest had thrown its plunder. It might have been dropped overboard by a matelot in a passing ship, or it might even have been the best cap tally on some 'tiddley' cap which had floated clear from the bottom of the sea. It reminded me that, not far from here, H.M.S. *Laforay* had gone down about thirteen years ago. There had been friends of mine aboard her and I had been laughing and drinking with them in Naples only two days before she sank. An air lifted over the rocks and suddenly I felt cold. There was no point in taking the tally back with me, and I left it among the seaweed and the fragments of cork and weevilled wood.

As I swam back I saw Janet come on deck, lower a bucket over the side and begin sluicing down the fo'c'sle.

'Anybody about?' she called as I came up by the bows and grasped the cable.

'Seems to be deserted,' I said. 'There's a boat, as you can see, but that's all. There may be some other cottages behind the rocks.'

You get those days in autumn that neither the summer nor even the spring can equal. The temperature at midday was seventy-five, and a light air stirred off the land and drew out to sea. A few threads of smoke marked cottages and farmhouses, but no one moved in the buildings on the shore.

After lunch we both swam, and I fished along the rocks while Janet stretched in the sun on the beach. Then I went out further beyond the second rock of I Faraglioni. There were a number of fish out there like small wrasse, and I tried for one or two but they knew me as dangerous and made off quickly. It suggested that other underwater fishermen had worked this bay quite recently, or else that all the fish in the Mediterranean were getting wary. But sometimes on the south coast I had been able to take fish which came up gently and almost placed themselves on my spear. They had never seen underwater man before, and I felt guilty then because I destroyed a kind of innocence. In most places, that had long since gone, and on the Riviera or in the Balearic islands, the fish were off like lightning the minute a man came down into their world. I never fished except to take what we needed to eat.

A rowing boat stood in from sea while I was off the point. There were three men in it and they asked me, 'What luck?'

'There are some flatfish on the bottom,' I said, 'but too deep for me —about ten metres.'

Twenty feet was about the most I could make and still have any reserves of air in my lungs to pursue a fish. These were just out of range.

'That is our boat on the beach,' they said. 'We are coming to tow it round to Castellammare.'

'I wondered to whom it belonged. No one lives here?'

'It is the tunny fishery stores. In the season many stay here. But now there is only a guardian of the stores and he lives a field back.'

'You are going to Castellammare today?' I asked.

'No,' said the coxswain. 'We shall stay here tonight and go round in the morning.'

'We are also going there in the morning,' I said. 'We can give you a tow if you wish.'

'So many thanks. That would help us greatly. What kind of engine have you?'

'A small English diesel,' I said.

'We are buying an engine for this boat,' said the coxswain. 'Not diesel, benzine. We will make better fishing then.'

'It is difficult in the winter without an engine,' said one of the men at the oars. 'Much work!'

He laughed and made the gesture of a man rowing in a heavy sea. He had the deep chest and the high ridge of muscle along the shoulders that comes from years over the loom of an oar.

Later that evening we watched the glow of their driftwood fire in the far corner of the beach. The old watchman had finally turned up and had given them permission to sleep in one of the buildings. They had some *bacalao* with them, the dried cod which is part of the staple diet in the winter months, and they were boiling it in an old dixie the watchman had loaned them. They had politely refused our offer of any other food, but had accepted a half-bottle of wine. It was a small-enough gift, for the wine we drank aboard rarely cost more than one-and-six a litre. For three shillings in the fishermen's bars you could have enough to make your head sing. With the exercise and the fresh air and the hot sun you soon sweated it out, though, and it did not stick in your liver and bones the way it did in the cold north. I don't think the word 'gout' occurs in the language.

As we sat on deck and drank our coffee the moon came up.

It was one of those still clear nights that you get in autumn. The moon was waxing, and beyond the bright curve of its arms you could see the shadow of the old moon.

> I saw the new moon late yestreen
> Wi' the auld moon in her arm;
> And if we gang to sea, master,
> I fear we'll come to harm. . . .

That might be true in Scotland. If you got a night up there as crisp and clear as this it would very likely mean that high wind was coming. But not here.

The fire on the beach flickered. Sometimes it burned green from the salt in the wood they were using, and every now and then, when they threw on another stick or log, a shower of sparks went up. A current of air drove the smell of wood smoke towards us.

'Winter soon,' I said.

'Another year gone.'

'Not a wasted one.'

For one year we had been able to say at almost every moment, 'Now I am alive.'

The vertical sides of I Faraglioni were austere under the moon. The one nearest the shore looked more and more like a ruined castle. Sometimes one of the men would be caught in the glow from the fire, and his shadow would loom gigantic on the white walls behind.

'I think I'll go for a swim,' I said.

The water was almost the same temperature as at noon and I swam slowly away from the boat, watching the shifting brightness of the phosphorescence in front of my arms. When I climbed back aboard, flickers of light ran off my skin and vivid specks flashed in the pool of water on deck. I was glad I had framed the day with a swim—and I knew that this day would stay with me.

WINTER

Hic tamen hanc mecum poteras requiescere noctem
fronde super viridi; sont nobis mitia poma,
castaneae molles et pressi copia lactis;
et iam summa procul villarum culmina fumant
maioresque cadunt altis de montibus umbrae.

Virgil. Eclogue I

But you could surely stay with me here for just a night, with fresh leaves for a couch? I have ripe apples, soft sweet chestnuts and a good store of cheese. And look, already from those farmyard roofs the evening smoke is rising, and the shadows lengthen from the mountain tops.

TWENTY

THE small fishing village of Mondello lies a little west of Palermo. In the summer it is a resort for the Palermitans, but by the end of autumn the beach and the white villas are deserted. The village goes back again to the fishermen, and by day the small quay is draped with their nets. The men sit out in the sunshine, holding the thick tarred webs between their toes and making them good from the chafe and wear of the sea. There is a small church at the village end of the quay. In the morning, from about four o'clock onward, there are always fishermen going in and out of it, leaving their oars and gear on the steps. Some of them are asking for favours before they put to sea, and others, whose feet are still spongy from the slop of bilge water all night long, are giving thanks for their catch. It was in Mondello that we first met Gaspare.

It was our first morning there, and I was sitting out on the upper deck stitching the canvas cover of a fender. It was a soft day, although it had been quite cold when we woke, and for the first time since January we had porridge for breakfast. There had been lots of fishermen along for a chat with us and the usual crowd of children. They were well mannered here, unlike some places in the south—Sciacca, for instance, where they would have the rivets out of the ship's side unless you had a local watchman aboard.

'*Scusi, signore* . . .'

I looked round. He was an old fisherman, grey-haired, in a faded blue shirt and canvas trousers. He was about medium height but seemed a little taller because of his leanness. His neck was like sun-dried leather and his arms were stringy with muscle. He had a good face and a gentle smile.

'Good morning,' I said. 'We just got in, last night. This is a beautiful small harbour.'

'Yes, Mondello is beautiful. This is my home town. I am born here, and married here, and live here always.'

'Come aboard,' I said. 'Would you care to have a look over the boat?'

'Many thanks. With your permission.'

He sat down on the jetty and dipped his feet over the side to wash off the sand and dust, then swung himself easily into the cockpit. I had not bothered to put out the gangway.

'What a beautiful little yacht.' He ran his hand over the goose-neck tiller. 'What is her name? I see it on the stern there but I cannot read it. Is it English?'

'Dutch,' I said. 'She is a Dutch boat, but we are English. '*Moeder de Gans*' it says on the stern, '*Mamma Occa*' in Italian, '*Mother Goose*' in English.'

Janet came out of the saloon with dustpan and brush, and he got to his feet, apologizing to the lady for being in the way. He was called Gaspare and he was a fisherman. He worked in his cousin's boat—that was it lying over there in the corner—and he had really come aboard to tell the signore that I would be better to anchor a little further out.

'This afternoon or evening comes a sirocco,' he said. 'At this time of the year it is very fierce. The wind comes over the mountains behind Mondello—whoosh! The harbour is agitated—the anchor drags—and perhaps you damage your little boat on the jetty.'

There was a lot of high cirrus coming over the island from the south and he pointed to it.

'See the clouds, signore! It will be very hot this afternoon and the wind strong as a lion.'

'It'll mean putting the dinghy in the water if we go further out,' I said to Janet. 'That's a bore, but better than having to shift in a hurry.'

The fishermen were not always reliable with their wind and weather forecasts. Quite often they had tried to dissuade us from putting to sea when there was nothing more than a good sailing breeze blowing. They were unfamiliar with yachts, and they tended to judge a boat's seaworthiness entirely by its size. A big, crank old schooner, leaking at every seam, they would designate as 'safe to go to sea in', but they would look at *Mother Goose*—no longer than their own open boats—and say: 'All right on a fine summer day, signore—but not when the wind really blows.' But with Gaspare I felt at once that his advice was sound. He had that old-fashioned, canny, reliable look you find in Scots fishermen. He spoke in a grating, salt-rimed voice, and the words came slowly, with none of the quicksilver vivacity of the Latin.

He gave us a hand out into the middle of the harbour and I dropped anchor where he advised. We had only just finished when the outriders of the sirocco were with us. A long mustard-coloured cloud began to lift over the inland hills and the air grew hot. I rowed the old man ashore and he showed me where his cottage was, a few yards down the street past the chapel.

'I hope to see you this evening,' I said.

'I think it will blow too hard for you to come ashore,' he replied. 'When you get back, make the dinghy well fast or take it on board. You will be safe where you are.'

Soon after, the wind began to come in hot hard blasts off the land. It was full of the dust and parched earth of Sicily. At the turn of the year those siroccos are more like a North African khamsin than anything else. The heat in them is blistering and they fling the hot earth like pepper in your eyes.

The sky was darkened and through the driving cloud the sun gleamed every now and then, red-faced and sullen. The dust was in our eyes and ears and mouths. It sprinkled our food, crunched under foot, and our skins were gritty to the touch. It blew all afternoon and the sun set orange and green beyond the huddled roof-tops of Mondello. The lights from the cafés, bars, and houses wore yellow haloes, like lights seen through a fog.

We kept anchor watches all night. That meant sitting below, hot and dusty, listening to the thunder of the wind in the rigging, and going out every quarter of an hour to check that the anchor was not dragging. Up on deck the wind really hit you, and it was strange how fiery it was on the skin. I had to hold on to the coach-roof handrails as I struggled forward, moving cautiously from mast to anchor winch, and so to the forestay. Then I switched on the torch and tried to see how the cable was lying. The harbour was wiry with broken waves and their chop and sizzle was loud up in the bows. I could tell, though, from the shore lights that the anchor was still holding and that the boat had not moved. It was good to go below again, have another cup of coffee and pick up a book. Down below there was that feeling of reassurance which a few personal possessions give you.

It was still blowing at dawn and the sea beyond the breakwater was a mass of foam. The air was a little clearer and we could see the quay astern of us and the nearest houses. We looked sadly at *Mother Goose*. She was stained ochre all over, and mustard tears wept down her varnish and paintwork. Small drifts of sand and earth were gathered in every corner, and the inside of the dinghy was lined with orange mud where the bilge water had slopped over the dust.

'You should see your face!' said Janet. 'It's a kind of nicotine colour
—with just your eyes sticking out. You look like a dissipated owl!'

'You should yours!' I said. 'I've got a mouth like the bottom of a
birdcage, I think I'll clean my teeth.'

'Let's have grapefruit for breakfast—that should freshen us up.'

In the late afternoon the wind began to ease, and soon after that
Gaspare came pulling out to us. During the past twenty-four hours it had
been too rough for any rowing boats to move in the harbour and they
were all drawn up on the beach. Gaspare's was the first to be launched.

'By tomorrow—no more wind,' he said. 'I just came to see if you or
the lady needed anything. Bread or pasta or *bacalao*?'

'We'd like to go ashore and have a bath,' I said. 'But would it be
possible for you to watch the boat for us?'

I knew there was quite a big hotel in Mondello, so it was safe to talk
about having a bath. We had been longing for one all morning.

'Yes, surely. I'll look after the little boat for you,' he said. 'But there is
no fear. If the anchor did not move during the night she will not move
now.'

We were lucky at the hotel. They were closing next week after the
season, and—yes, they had a bathroom in operation. There had been
some English staying there only a fortnight ago, Mr. and Mrs. Calthrop
from London—we must surely know them—and they had taken baths
every morning and every night. I knew what the hotel people were
thinking, but were too polite to say to our faces: 'That's what makes the
British so sad and long-faced. They wash away all the natural oils from
the skin. And that's why they have less children than the Italians—the
constant hot water saps their virility.' (Among the poorer people of
Sicily and southern Italy it was an article of belief that the size of the
family proved the husband's manhood. The fact that the English, Americans, and French had families of only one or two was entirely due to lack
of this saving virtue.)

Hot baths are always one of the problems if you live in a small boat,
but it was not one that had worried us greatly in that clement world. We
swam once or twice almost every day, and we could always have a stand-
up wash in the cabin. Most places we went to there were no baths in any
case, but we did not get dirty living that life. The boat was clean, the air
was clean, and usually the only thing that powdered our bodies or clothes
was the sand from some lonely cove. It was easy to keep pace with our
own washing: we wore few clothes, and shirts and shorts would dry in an
hour on deck. But a hot bath was a luxury and our last had been in

Syracuse some four weeks back. Ashore, in a big city with hot water always on tap, one forgets what a bath feels like.

That night, for once, we were really dirty, coated with dust and sand, and tired after our anchor watch. I lay a long time in the bath, and read an old paper-back. I was drugged by the hot, steamy air and the drowsy movement of the water over my body, but I was snapped out of it by Janet knocking on the door.

'Don't be too long! I've finished, and I think the manager's worried in case you've drowned.'

They charged us nearly ten shillings a head for our baths, but they were worth it. Wine was cheaper than hot water there, but sometimes water is almost as good. We both put on clean shore-going clothes with creases to my trousers and a starched flared skirt to Janet's dress. We had an old-fashioned flat-iron aboard *Mother Goose* and we kept our shore clothes almost as well as if we had lived in a house.

We sat in the hotel bar and had a few Martinis and some fat green olives. It was strange to feel 'City Slicker' and 'civilized' after so long away from that world.

'I must say you appreciate it when you come back to it,' I said.

The wind was dying with the nightfall and the clouds had gone out to sea, way on towards the north. The sirocco would be heavy over the Bay of Naples by now. It would have picked up plenty of moisture crossing the Tyrrhenian, and the wind that had been hot and dry for us would be trailing white clouds like a sweat-robe over the heights of Capri.

Three days later we put out from Mondello and set course for Palermo. Gaspare came with us 'just for the ride'. He would help us berth the boat in a quiet corner he knew, where we would be near the main road to town, and where the people were reliable. It was a bright day and there was enough wind to keep the sails heavy and full.

'A beautiful little boat,' said Gaspare. 'At first, when you tell me that you come from England in her, just you and the lady, why . . . But now I feel how she is a real boat for the sea. Not just for a summer day.'

We passed close under the stiff, shining sides of Monte Pellegrino.

'Santa Rosalia,' said Gaspare, pointing to the mountain's brown head. 'La Santuzza.'

Santa Rosalia was a slightly obscure Norman virgin who was martyred in the twelfth century. She did not occupy much place in Sicilian affections until the great plague of 1624 when her relics were carried through the city and the plague abated. But since then she had performed thousands of miracles and her fame had eclipsed all her island rivals, even Sant' Agata of Catania. Her shrine lies high on the peak of Monte Pellegrino in a grotto where once the Sicilians most probably worshipped the great Earth-Mother. The uncharitable (including an Italian doctor who wrote a treatise on his findings) have maintained that the bones are those of a goat which died of old age or exposure on the mountain. But it makes little difference whether they are genuine, or who she was, even. 'La Santuzza', the people call her, and their belief in her has charged the mountain cave with power.

The wind came fresher as we rounded the point. There was a steamer coming in from the north, the Naples–Palermo packet most likely, and there were many small sailing boats broadcast over the bay.

'Behold—the city!' said Gaspare.

It lay spread out in front of us, matt-gold under the sun, with the darkness of orange and lemon groves circling around it.

We altered course and took the wind over our quarter, and the wake began to murmur and shine. We could see the masts and rigging of many ships in the harbour and a haze of blue smoke trailed over the dockyard. The buildings on the sea-front were coming up fast now, defining themselves in the clear light of early winter.

'La Conca d'Oro!'

Gaspare gestured to the green arm of fruit trees that embraced the city. Behind it rose the long foot-hills of the Madonie mountains and on the horizon the far-off peaks were cold and blue.

TWENTY-ONE

I WAS up early. There were lots of things I had to do before starting work with the film company, and I wanted to buy some food, for there would be no time later on in the day. *Mother Goose* was lying alongside one of the big French tunny-fishing boats which had been converted to look like eighteenth-century men-of-war and which were generally known as 'the galleons'. Her high poop, garlanded with plaster-of-Paris cupids and trumpets, loomed right over me as I sat in the cockpit and had a shave. The Maltese cook aboard her was awake, drinking tea out of a half-pint glass the way they do in Malta, and he called down to me:

'*Bon jour!*'

'What time are you going out?' I asked.

'About ten,' he said. 'Both ships are going.'

We were going to film one of the battle scenes today, out in the bay, and I only hoped it would not blow too hard. Those big ships were almost uncontrollable when the wind got them on the beam. They looked authentic, though, and would look more so on the screen, but they were never meant to take a real wind.

Getting the job had been a stroke of luck. A day or so after we had come into Palermo a friend of mine from Malta had suddenly turned up.

'Want to make some money?' he asked.

'Of course,' I said. 'We could always eat better.'

'I thought you'd gone off to Greece,' he said. 'If I'd known you were still loafing round Sicily I'd have sent you the word a week ago.'

He was the naval adviser to the film unit, and within a few minutes he had made me his assistant. That, as I soon found out, meant getting paid for pleasure. All I had to do was drive a fast diesel yacht round and about, and act as general transport for director, stars, cameramen, and anything or anyone who needed taking from one part of Palermo Bay to another. They were making most of the film down at Arenella, a fishing village on the outskirts of the city which the company had more or less taken over. Most of the battle scenes and heroic deeds of derring-do were being shot in the bay. It was a pleasant way to earn a little money and we could certainly use it. It would help us over the winter in Palermo and we would put a little aside for *Mother Goose*'s refit in the spring.

So I was up at six on a crisp morning in early winter, watching the night clouds lift off the hills behind the city, and hearing the clatter of the carts as they came into town down the main road a few yards away. We were lying right across from the dockyard quarter and, from where I sat, I could see one of the alleys with the washing flapping overhead and children playing in the dust. A water-seller with a brass canister strapped on his back went by and called out in a scratched voice: 'Water! Beautiful water! More beautiful than the soul of my heart!'

After I had finished shaving I climbed the rope ladder that hung down from the galleon's main deck some twenty foot above us and went ashore. There were one or two fishermen and dockside loungers standing around the foot of the gangway-plank looking up at the ship. They were probably hoping to get taken on as extras or crew, but all the jobs had gone long ago. Down at Arenella, where most of the work was done, the whole of the population was in it one way or another. The fishermen were all disguised as pirates during the day, while their wives and daughters worked for the wardrobe department, scrubbed floors, cooked meals, or gave the houses a coat of white-wash.

'Hey, Captain——' they all started up as I came ashore.

'Not me,' I said, 'the captain's still asleep. I don't think there are any jobs left.'

They sat down again to wait, while I went on up the dockyard, over the railway tracks, and across to the bridge where the bread cart was standing. It was a well-painted cart with scenes from Orlando's life on each of its two main panels, and a carving over the stern of the Flight into Egypt. The donkey was a good piece of work and so was old Joseph, leaning on a staff, while the Virgin in a blue robe followed him, holding the Child. Joseph was looking over his shoulder as if he expected pursuers.

By the end of the winter I would know the bread-seller and his son quite well, but we were still strangers as yet. He thought I came from the film company and he tried to charge me accordingly. I bought four rolls for our lunch and then went across to the tobacconist's where they also sold stamps and daily papers. It was run by an old woman and her daughter. The daughter was about eighteen with fine eyes and a big strong body.

144

The other evening her young man had been with her and I had watched a typical Sicilian courtship. The mother was seated in her chair behind the counter busily knitting while at the same time she kept a beady eye on her daughter. The couple were seated on straight-back wooden chairs side by side in the far corner of the shop. The girl was looking modestly at the ground and her young man was clearly telling her that she was sweeter than the finest grapes from Monreale. They were holding hands—that was allowed—but I noticed that when he tried to press his knee against hers (while the mother was serving me with cigarettes), the girl had quickly leaned her body away from his. Her young man was a good deal older than her—the men were often in their thirties before they could afford to marry—and I knew that he would only be allowed one kiss before he left, and that the kiss would be given in front of Mother.

This morning only the old lady was in the shop. I bought two packets of Nazionali, some wax matches, and a *Giornale* from her. She took my money, crossed herself, and put it in the till. I was an early bird and her first customer of the day. I knew that, because devout shop-owners always crossed themselves in thanks when they took their first money.

I turned right outside her shop and went on up the main street into town. Bar-owners and shopkeepers were already busy in that quarter, sluicing down the pavements and getting ready for the day. Coffee was being roasted at the shop on the corner, and just beyond it the smell of baking bread swirled out of a basement. I stopped by a cart loaded with fruit, and bought some mandarins for our lunch. Then I bought some cheese and two thick slices of tunny from the grocer. He cut the tunny off the big slab on the counter and weighed each slice carefully, throwing on a few broken flakes to bring the needle exactly to weight.

When I got back to the dockyard Gaspare had already arrived. He and Janet and one of the Maltese sailors from the galleon had moved *Mother Goose* further down the jetty so that she was not in the way when the galleon put out. Gaspare had got himself a job with the film company and, when the boats were laid up for the winter, he was going to remain as night watchman for them. In the meantime he was also working a little for us in *Mother Goose*. I showed him what I wanted done that day, some fenders repaired and the canvas cover for the forehatch resewn. He was a good hand with a palm and needle, neat and painstaking, and I left him sitting cross-legged like a tailor on the fo'c'sle in the pale sunlight.

Janet and I walked along to where the motor boat lay. She was a forty-foot launch with twin diesels and a speed of about sixteen knots.

After having got used to *Mother Goose* under power, with her slow-running engine and her off-centre propeller, it felt strange to have so much power under one's belt. The engines started with a roar and I let them run at full boost for a bit to get everything easy and flowing. The cameramen started to arrive, then the director, and then a number of 'pirates'. These were not locals, but English stunt-men. They had a job on that day to row across the bay in a long-boat and make an attack on the smaller galleon. I could see it out there already, going slowly along under power while her hands were getting up sails.

'All ready?' The director was American, taut and nervous, with a smile reserved for the better-paid. That morning he was more tense than usual. He was having a little trouble with one of the male leads who had been threatening to throw his hand in.

'All ready,' I said, and we cast off and went on up the harbour with the long-boat in tow behind us. When we were about half a mile away from the smaller galleon the pirates climbed into their boat and began to row away. There was a slight swell that morning, nothing much, but long and easy, running in round Cape Zaffarano.

'Those pirates don't look so good,' Janet said quietly. 'For "deep-sea killers" they look pretty unused to rowing.'

That was true. They were splashing and floundering along like a bunch of business men on a Bank Holiday outing. The director didn't seem to notice, though, and the cameramen said everything was fine.

'Bum pirates,' I said to my friend who had dropped into the wheelhouse after giving the director some advice about 'not photographing the galleon until she has all her sails up'.

'I know,' he said. 'But we can't use the locals today. It's a stunt-man's job. When they get up near the galleon, one of the characters is going to open fire with a culverin and then—boom!—the coxswain presses a tit in the boat and up they go.'

'Rather them than me.'

I looked through the binoculars at the long-boat. Something was wrong over there. They had stopped rowing and the boat was drifting beam on in the swell.

'What the hell?'

'Better close them,' he said, 'and see what goes on.'

The pirates were slumped over the looms of the oars and one of them was leaning right out of the boat. Only the coxswain looked normal—and we could hear him shouting as we came alongside. I cut the engines and we idled up so that they were in our lee.

'A bloody fine bunch!' he called up.

'It's the —— swell!' groaned the bowman.

The pirates were throwing their hearts up and the bilges were sour. The film director was worried.

'We can't go on if these men are so ill,' he said.

Paddy, the coxswain, was a big Irishman with a grey beard. He gave me a grin.

'They're not ill really, are they?' he said. 'It's just that they didn't believe you last night when you said this local *vino* was strong! They'll be all right in a few minutes, sorr!' he called to the director.

Five minutes later we were all set for the big shot as the long-boat came up under the stern of the galleon. The cameras were turning, everyone was busy, and I was keeping the launch about twenty yards off.

'Any minute now . . .'

We saw the puff of smoke as the galleon's stern-chaser fired and—wham! There was a real fountain as the boat went up. Lumps of wood went flying in all directions and men were falling over the side, and there was old Paddy still sitting in the stern, with the boat going down under him.

'Perfect!'

The director was happy and the cameramen were happy. We closed the boat quickly and threw scramble-nets over the side. One of the pirates was floating bottom upwards on the water, like a fish that has been dynamited to the surface. As we hauled him aboard he began to twitch and stir. One of his mates was massaging his thigh and swearing steadily and with great fluency. Paddy was laughing, but the rest seemed to be hopping mad.

'Beautiful!' said the director. 'That's one scene we shan't have to shoot again.'

'Fine!' said the cameraman. 'Nothing phoney about that. Just like a war film. How'd you manage it, boys?'

'That bastard'—one of the pirates pointed to Paddy—'double-crossed us!'

Paddy came into the wheelhouse and helped himself to a drink.

'Dick's okay,' he said. 'You know—the kid who was a bit stunned. None of 'em are hurt. Sure, they really earned their danger money today.'

'What happened?' I said. 'It looked good. Your boat went up as if you'd been hit by a real cannon-ball.'

'Well, the first thing,' he said, 'was—that the explosives department really put a charge in there today! You know we were taking the micky out of them the other morning when those cannons just gave a pouf! like wet squibs—they weren't going to have that happen again. The other thing was, I'd fixed it with the boys that I was going to count "one—two —three" slowly—and fire after I'd said "three". Well, you know how it is. They are all rowing along, looking at me and easing about as if they'd got hot pants. They've been sick anyway and they're not feeling so good, so I know that when I start counting, half of them will be over the side when I get to "two" and the other half at "three". Now that won't look good with everyone bailing out before the bang. I don't want to spend another day out here and it means fixing up another boat if we wreck this one—so I start counting. "One", I says, and they're looking white and nervy. Then I press the tit before I get to two!'

'They'll kill you,' I said.

'Oh no, they won't. We can go off swimming now or on the booze. They won't kill me—they'll buy me a drink!'

There were many days like that, good-humoured days, and more often than not something happened. There was the time when the leading lady was supposed to be having a row with the hero. As she turned away, 'in impetuous fury', her dress caught on a nail sticking out from one of the dummy cannons. The cameras were still turning as, with a long ripping sigh, her skirt came off. Then there was the time when the male lead slipped backwards in a duelling scene and fell down a gangway. The film called for just such a scene, but for insurance reasons they kept a well-paid stand-in to do that job.

The film people regarded the Sicilian fishermen, extras, and all the rest of the local employees, as 'hicks from the sticks' and 'peasants from the deep south'.

'They're so dumb it hurts,' said the starlet (she took the part of an ingenuous victim of rape).

'They're not so dumb,' I said.

The 'simple peasantry' and the illiterate fishermen made rings round the sophisticated film-makers. Almost every fisherman managed to get his boat damaged in some way or another so that he had to be fully compensated—which often meant that he ended up with two boats, where he had started with one. In Arenella they were stacking away diesel fuel, rope and cordage, paint and varnish, electric-light bulbs, bales of cloth, drums of oil, and even a small diesel charging-plant, which mysteriously 'disappeared' one day.

Gaspare was full of admiration for the drinking and sexual prowess of one of the male stars.

'He is like a bull,' he said to me one evening. 'Is it the whisky which gives him his force, or is it the ladies who give him his thirst? Of course, he eats better than us, meat every day.'

Among the Sicilians meat was a luxury, eaten once a week, or among the very poor only on special occasions. Their diet of pasta and fruit and fish was a healthy one, though, and the olive oil gave them good skins and clear eyes. I had once offered Gaspare some butter but he rejected it politely and firmly. He found the idea of eating it or cooking with it distasteful.

'Animal fat, signore,' he said, 'it is not good for you. And then if you fry something in it, pouf! What a stink! Olive oil is clean and natural.'

'The women in England and America have much freedom,' he said to me one day. It was his oblique comment on a young blonde who had just gone by with her arm round a fisherman.

'They are not happy, though,' he went on, 'they do not respect men the way women do in Sicily.'

That reminded me of another comment the starlet had made to me.

'Hell,' she said, rolling her big dark eyes. 'Who'd be a woman in this island? Pregnant year in, year out. And the men just lolling about in the cafés while the women stay indoors.'

She was right that the women stayed mostly indoors. The Moorish influence on Sicilian custom was still strong, and that was particularly true of the villages in the north. When you went through the streets, back in the Giuliano country round Montelepre, you would see women sitting in the doorways, with their backs turned to the road so that their faces and legs could not be seen by passers-by. Except for the rich cosmopolitan set, who had houses in Rome and had travelled, you would find little visible sign that the Sicilian woman was anything other than a breeding machine. But that was only on the surface. They had far more power over their men's lives and over their families than in any western country. 'The Mother' was the backbone of Sicily, just as the Virgin Mary—or Santa Rosalia in Palermo—was a good deal more important than Jesus Christ. Sicily was one island where the Galilean had not conquered; he had just been quietly absorbed. 'He was not much of a saint,' as Gaspare remarked once. 'He never did many miracles. And he behaved badly to his mother, too.'

It was Gaspare who had pointed the contrast for me between the casual visitor's idea of the Sicilian woman and her true position. He had flapped a copy of a weekly magazine at me one day and asked me to read one of the articles.

'Is that really so?' he said when I had looked at it.

The article described the daily life of an English working man, and the difference between him and his Italian counterpart. What astonished Gaspare was the statement that: 'In England the wife often does not know exactly how much her husband makes. He gives her whatever he thinks fit for her housekeeping money.'

'I think it's sometimes the case,' I said, hedging a bit.

In Sicily, as I knew, it was not so. I had been to Gaspare's home in Mondello one night just after he had been paid. His wife and his old mother of ninety were sitting in the living-room when we came in, their hands folded in their laps, in front of the scrubbed wooden table. Gaspare had taken a pile of notes and coins from his pocket and had put it down in front of them. His wife counted through them and noticed that it was about ten lire short (the old man had stopped for a couple of drinks on the way). She said nothing in front of me, a stranger, but I knew by the tightening of her lips that he would get a curtain lecture later on. Then she had sorted out the money into a number of small piles—rent, food, clothing, household equipment—until at the end there were only a few lire left on the table. Not much—five or six shillings. She swept them in Gaspare's direction with the back of her hand. That was his pocket money for the week. Yet, that same evening perhaps, the young starlet would see Gaspare lounging at a café table in his best blue suit, and would be even more confident that Sicily was a country that was fine and dandy if you were a man.

After three weeks the film was finished and the company began to pack up its gear and head back for America.

'You staying here over the winter?' the director asked me. He was a bit incredulous. 'Well, each man to his own taste, I guess. I'm certainly glad I'm not. Boy, they're just a bunch of "winos" and rogues here. They clip you at every turn.'

'You can't get a local piece of tail,' said one of the cameramen. 'They lock up the women when they see you coming.'

'Naturally.'

Only Paddy and a few of the stunt-men seemed to have enjoyed themselves. They had gone drinking in the local bars and had made friends with some of the fishermen and shoreside dock-workers. The Sicilians had quickly seen that these men were something like themselves —better paid, but working men all the same.

Janet and I had one last job—to take the launch, with a Maltese engineer aboard, down to Syracuse and leave her there. There was a farewell party the night we sailed, with dancing up at the big hotel, and a lot of drinks and noise. We left about four o'clock in the morning, and the engineer had a head like a balloon so that he could just about check the tanks, start up the motors, and pass out.

'I'll take her first,' I said to Janet.

As soon as we were clear of the harbour I opened her right up, and our stern settled down and our bows lifted. In a few minutes we were creaming along at sixteen knots with our wake rolling out a broad swath far astern of us. The slipped sea from each quarter went back at a slight angle so that their tracks crossed about a hundred yards astern and then went away in two deep wedges. I eased her as we came round Cape Zaffarano, for there were a number of fishing boats out working with nets and lines.

The sun began to lift over Sicily just as we were passing Cefalù. I could see the bald head of the cape shining in the new light, and mist was pouring down the far side of it into the village. We passed a coaster a little further on and the crew came out on deck and gave us a cheer. We must have looked good riding along on our crest of foam, but somehow that kind of boat held little pleasure for me. The thunder of the great diesels, and the buck and bounce of the boat, made it seem more like driving a racing car than being at sea. Stray currents, and shifts of wind, and the smell of the night air, and the silence of the sea—these were things you knew nothing about in a fast power boat.

We went through the Straits of Messina with the *Scendente* under our tail, so that we were doing about eighteen knots. Homer was forgotten again, and any whirlpools or broken water went by unnoticed. We dropped Messina astern, and then there was Etna coming out of the bright morning, high on our right hand. There was a good deal of snow on the peak, more than when we had come by in *Mother Goose*, and the breeze that stirred off the land had the scent of ice on it. All down the foothills and back of Riposto the land was green with the vines and fruit trees.

Janet took the wheel while I had a sleep. When I came out again it was round about noon, and there was Acireale on the beam with its white houses huddled along the cliff face. Astern of us Taormina was bathed in sunlight, Catania was smoky on the bow, and we could just see Porto Brucoli coming up ahead.

'To think we took nearly two weeks meandering up this coast,' said Janet.

In the late afternoon we boomed round Castello Maniace into the calmness of Syracuse and dropped anchor off the main promenade. The first strollers were just appearing. In an hour or so, everyone would be making the *passegiata* in their best suits and dresses, and the lights would begin to twinkle from the cafés and bars. We would have a hot bath in the big hotel and we would find Francu and Pietru. We would spend a leisured evening talking, and watching the darkness come down over the harbour.

TWENTY-TWO

EVERY morning when we opened the hatch we looked out on the noble bay. On the one hand Monte Pellegrino was stark against the sky, and on the other—far in the distance—Monte Zaffarano stooped like an eagle into the sea.

Even in winter it was clear on most mornings and the days were often warm and still. Sometimes there was snow on the Madonie mountains, yet in the Conca d'Oro, the fertile Golden Shell which enriches the city, the oranges were hanging like lanterns in the green night of their leaves.

Oranges and tangerines had always been something I had associated with childhood and Christmas. I said as much one day to Giulio, a Sicilian friend, as we were walking through the narrow alleys of the dockyard quarter.

'To me they are the smell of poverty.' He waved his hand towards the dark doorway out of which every now and then burst hordes of brown, bare-foot children.

In every street or alley there were small shrines, sometimes only an oleograph of the Madonna behind glass, but in other places a statue with protecting bars around it, or a full-length painting of a saint. Candles and oil-lamps, *ex-votos* and testimonials clustered around the more popular saints. Some shrines had a sad forgotten air, with only a faded bunch of flowers to show that anyone still remembered them.

Religion in Sicily is humanized and very personal—one man's saint may be another man's poison. There is the story of a man who was work-ing on a public building, high up on a scaffolding overlooking the city. Suddenly he slipped and fell. As he tumbled through the air he called desperately to his patron saint, 'St. John—save me!' A huge hand reached from the sky, grasped him by the coat collar, and stopped his fall. 'Which John?' boomed a deep voice. 'The—the Apostle,' quavered the workman. The hand let go and he plummeted downwards. It had been St. John the Baptist.

In Sicily religion is often as realist as in the ancient world. A bargain is struck in return for favours, and if they do not materialize then the promised lire and candles are not forthcoming either. A friend of Gaspare remarked one day that he had promised candles to Santa Rosalia if he had a good season fishing. It had been a bad one, so he had now concluded the same bargain with Saint Damian. 'It should work better this time,' he said. 'After all, he was a man.'

The memory of the ancient world is not confined to gods alone. Many legends and superstitions linger in Palermo, some of them relics of long-dead conquerors and other faiths. I had a good example that same morning.

'I must leave a message for one of our workmen,' Giulio said. He took me down one of the narrow side streets, and knocked at a door. The woman who opened it was holding a small boy in her arms. The child looked up at me and smiled, so I smiled back. It was then that I noticed the mother making a curious gesture with her right hand. It was clenched, but the forefinger and the little finger protruded. As we walked on I imitated it.

'What does that mean, Giulio?'

He laughed. 'Your blue eyes! She thought you were putting the evil eye on the child. Blue-eyed people are supposed to be able to do that, you know.'

The gesture of 'The Horns' (which here has nothing to do with cuckoldry) is an Arabic one and dates back to the Mohammedan occupation of the island. So do the bull's horns which are often nailed over doorways (like the horseshoe in England), and sometimes even fixed to the crosstrees of fishing boats' masts. Palm branches, relics from Palm Sunday, were the Christian contribution to warding off ill luck and evil spirits, and they too were sometimes secured to the masts of boats.

There were two worlds in Palermo, the rich and the poor. Giulio belonged to the rich and he was very conscious of it. His family went back almost as far as Julius Caesar, and apropos an English duke who was visiting the island, he said: 'Of course, his family were tradespeople at about the time we were adding the second wing to the country house at Bagheria.' (They had not so much money nowadays since the great estates had been split up. Also, like many of the nobility, they still regarded commerce and trade as something that 'one's position prevents one from indulging in'.)

We walked down the Via Roma for a coffee. Every morning Giulio would get up at about ten, spend at least an hour on his toilet, and then

154

stroll down to watch the world from a comfortable table. He was an amusing companion and he had great honesty. This morning he told me his story of the last days of the Italian resistance to the Allies. 'I was in command of an anti-aircraft battery in the south of Italy,' he said, 'and I was greatly worried. Night and day the Americans were bombing all round us. I had so much ammunition on the dump that I didn't know what to do.'

'Why not fire it off at them?' I said.

'Exactly. Of course I did that whenever any of them came near. But still I kept thinking, "If one of them ever does drop a bomb here we shall all go up in one big bang!" They were not very good bomb-aimers the Americans, you know. Although they are trying to hit my dump and my guns, they are only hitting the residential part of the town. "But one day," I think, "they are bound to hit me—by mistake." Well, just before we hear about the Armistice, I decide to stage an air-raid on my own. I call out my men, man all the guns and for nearly twelve hours we fire and fire into the sky. Finally we finish, and now I can feel quite confident that if we are killed it will only be bad luck, and nothing more. There is no ammunition dump left!'

Giulio left me to go back to the palazzo for lunch. It was a fine old building with a main shell that was sixteenth century and bits and pieces added on right up to the eighteen-thirties. Since then time had stopped. It might well have been an Irish country house which neither a rich Englishman nor a richer American had yet chanced upon and poured money into. There were always numbers of old servants scuttling from doors into mysterious unknown wings, or emerging from the private chapel. Giulio's family were kind people; if they had let off parts of the palace, they could have made money. Instead, there were these old retainers and innumerable aunts and stray relatives, one of whom had a passion for birds and her whole room was like a crazy sanctuary for canaries, budgerigars, and minas.

Giulio behind a mound of pasta was an amazing sight. Any English conception I might still have kept, that there was a polite way of eating it, finally went by the board. He would get his head down to the level of the top of the pile and shovel it away in an almost continuous movement.

'Eat it up,' he said to Janet and me one day. 'Don't you like it? Ah, I know you do—but you still can't get through pasta like I can.'

He was full of bounce that day, for he had put two old English women properly in their places the night before. They had been introduced to him by the Consul, and they were fine old county 'ladies' in tweeds and good brogues who loved Sicily but had had it all spoiled for them by the treatment of the animals.

'I explained to them,' said Giulio, 'the peasants and the cart drivers aren't deliberately cruel to their animals. Life here, though, is cruel to the human being—that's what these old virgins do not understand.'

'I hope you didn't call them that to their faces,' I said.

'Naturally not. Anyway, they are proud of their condition. But I did explain that, within his understanding of the way of life, the peasant is kind to his animals. Ah, if only they would worry about human beings first! I explained how an animal represented a lot of money to a country-man, and therefore he would not senselessly kick it or beat it to death. Of course he beats it occasionally, but then life beats him too. That's the way he sees it. Anyway, I failed to convince them—and they are report-ing the whole island to the R.S.P.C.A. when they go back. At that moment I am afraid I got a little annoyed. "Why should they come to my country," I said to myself, "and abuse it to my face?" There are many things in England, too, which could be better, and I tell them one. When I was last in London I said to them, the papers were full of stories about cruelty to children; about an English father beating his son to death, and about an English mother who burnt her small daughter's arm with a poker. Of course they both jumped at that and said: "Of course, these dreadful things do happen. But we have the National Society for the Pre-vention of Cruelty to Children to deal with them!" "Have you?" I said. "Well, then, let me tell you one thing—in Sicily we have no such society. And do you know why? There is no cruelty to children in my country!" They never spoke to me for the rest of the evening.'

I believed Giulio when he said there was no need for the N.S.P.C.C. I had been in some tough homes in the island, not in Palermo alone, but down in the south where conditions were even more primitive. One thing I had never seen was any sign of unkindness to children—not even the sudden slap or shout caused by strained nerves which happens in almost any English home. The Sicilians loved their children with a deep posses-sive love, and, especially if it was a boy, with a kind of animal adoration that was moving. I had visited people who lived in only two rooms with eight children, and the depth of family love might be called 'excessive' in our northern countries—but that was all.

A few days later an English ballet company visited Palermo. Giulio, hearing that the stage manager was a friend of mine, at once asked for an introduction to the dancers.

'You'll meet some of them if you come down to the boat tonight,' I said. 'Two or three of them are coming along to have a drink with us.'

'Ah, good. How kind of you.' He gave me a significant smile, and I knew that he would spend more time than usual on his toilet.

'I didn't know you cared for ballet, Giulio,' I said.

'Ah.' He looked at his nails. 'Dancers! You know . . .'

The pattern of life was Victorian, or almost eighteenth-century, for the Sicilian upper class, and so were many of their conceptions. I had no intention of disillusioning Giulio. He would find out for himself before the evening was out. I knew quite well that to him a dancer was a girl who displayed herself in order to find a rich lover. She was something designed for the nobleman's hours of ease. Not that Giulio was all that rich, but he was certainly titled, distinguished-looking, and he did have a part share, as it were, in the family palazzo.

He met the girls that evening and I heard him arrange to take one of them out to dinner after the show at the Teatro Massimo was over. It was evening dress there that night and the family boxes were crowded with smooth olive faces and fine jewellery. Giulio waved to us in the interval and he was smiling like a cat that sees a bowl of cream.

'Amuse yourself,' I said as we were making our goodbyes outside the theatre. 'Where are you taking the young lady to dinner?'

'To the Papagallo,' he said, 'and afterwards to show her my home and gardens. Well'—he consulted his watch—'*Ciaou*, Ernle.'

'*Ciaou*,' I said.

Janet laughed as we walked on home. 'The Papagallo! Giulio is really putting on the dog—he nearly always eats at home. That will set him back a bit. Does he know she's married?'

'Yes, I told him. But you know how he is—convinced of the old charm, and quite unconvinced by my telling him that even respectable women are dancers in England.'

Giulio was grave, even a little sour, the next day.

'You know,' he said thoughtfully as we sat taking our morning coffee, watching the smart women going up and down, and the bright traffic on the Via Roma, 'English women are cold!'

'Some of them,' I said.

'That little dancer—she is cold. And they are only here for two days more! I hardly have time to find another one.'

'I *did* tell you she was married,' I said.

He cocked a brown eye at me. 'Naturally. And I thought to myself,

"That is the action of a friend." You know that married women are always easier.'

That was the Sicilian convention, and you could no more change Giulio's mind on the subject than you could the two old English women on the treatment of animals in the island. As far as Giulio was concerned, unmarried girls were unapproachable. I had been to those parties in Palermo where the young girls sat quietly under their mother's eye, all of them in a half-circle at the far end of the room. I had been told the etiquette by Giulio: 'Kiss the hand of a married woman if you have been introduced to her before, but never kiss the hand of an unmarried girl.' Both in Giulio's class, and in Gaspare's, the young girls were kept under strict surveillance. It was expected that they should come innocent to their husband on the wedding night—and there would be the devil to pay if anything was missing. But once a woman was married, that was a different matter.

An English friend of mine had married a Sicilian and had been amused, as well as annoyed, when his wife told him that three of the Palermitan nobility had made her a proposition within two weeks of marriage. That was something which they would never have done before. But now it was assumed that she had only married for money and position in any case, and would be interested in a lover. As Giulio had so carefully explained to me, 'The appetite for love is awakened by the husband, but it is the lover who reaps the benefit.'

In almost everything Sicily is the reverse of England. That same afternoon the girl who had turned down Giulio, and four or five others from the ballet, decided to bathe off the beach near Mondello. It was the time of year when the locals considered that only a madman would bathe anyway, but I guess the temperature was nearer seventy than sixty so it seemed sensible to young women just arrived from mid-winter London. They wore bikinis.

'It is disgusting,' said Giulio as we watched them walk from their beach-hut down to the sea. 'You can see the navel—almost everything. It's uncivilized!'

The girls had their swim and then came out and lay on the beach. A few minutes later the first fisherman came by, carrying a net over his shoulder. He dropped it and stood and stared. Three or four youths came out of a cottage and joined him. They squatted down on their haunches like jackals round a carcase and stared. More fishermen came along. Within five minutes there was a crowd of thirty men sitting on the sand in a circle around the girls. Only one or two of the younger ones, who had a few words of English, tried a little conversation. The others said nothing but sat there in a kind of tense, hungry silence.

'Look!' said Giulio. 'They are deliberately enticing those men—and yet they are all cold, those English girls!'

It was not long before the almost savage absorption of thirty pairs of eyes proved too much, and the girls broke ranks and fled to the unwatched darkness of their bathing hut. None of the fishermen had ever seen women displaying themselves like that before. Even the married ones, most likely, had never seen their wives naked. It was probably the first occasion that any of them had ever seen a bare female belly and navel in their lives. Giulio, at any rate, had a laugh and a small revenge.

'They're all sex-starved, the men here,' one of the girls said to Janet afterwards. 'It's disgusting!'

So it was not easy to explain to the English that the Sicilians were pretty civilized in their way, nor to explain the other way round. The size of Sicilian families seemed absurd and pathetic to English visitors, and the lack of large families in England proved to the Sicilian the equally absurd and pathetic impotence of the English male. The elaborate wayside shrines and the barley-sugar baroque churches seemed to the English to prove that this was a miserable, priest-ridden society (which in some ways was true). On the other hand, Giulio thought that England was a country where a high standard of living was the ultimate aim of life, and where the churches were half-empty because no one had any real faith (which in some ways was also true).

Palermo was a city with two faces, its public and its private one. There are guide-books for the public face, and it is certainly handsome—more interesting than many of the better-known Italian beauties. Here in one city there is architecture from Carthaginian, Greek, Roman, and Moorish times, right up to the ripe splendour of eighteenth-century baroque. The pink domes of San Giovanni degli Eremiti floated like bubbles over the city, in the cloisters of Monreale fountains plashed, and in the Capucin catacombs the dead hung like dried fish in the darkness.

In the library of Giulio's home you could sit and never know that time had passed since 1830, when almost the last books had been bought. One day, as I was riffling through the pages of an old history of Palermo, a piece of paper floated out. I picked it up and looked at it idly—faded sepia handwriting on a letter headed 'Ravenna'.

'Ah, that's where it's got to.' Giulio peered over my shoulder. 'It's been missing for ages. I thought perhaps my brother had sold it when he last went to Rome.'

It was a letter from Byron to Giulio's great-grandfather, not a very long letter, written in a bored moment when he was beginning to tire of being a *cavaliere servente*. He was wondering then whether Greece or South America would best fill in the 'craving void' of ennui.

'What shall I do with it?' I said.

'Oh, better leave it where it lies. It's quite safe. There are several more, somewhere or other. I'd like you to look at them but I can't quite remember where they are.'

I put it back in the book. I expect it is still there.

'Let's go in the garden,' said Giulio. 'I think Janet's out there with my aunt.'

His aunt could speak no English and I knew that Janet would be listening to involved tales of people long dead, and to old family histories and intricate scandals. Mixed up with this would be passionate denunciations of the Protestants (there was one small Protestant church in Palermo), for Giulio's aunt, unlike the rest of the family, was given to proselytizing. An American had once stayed in the palace and had left behind a Protestant bible. Giulio's mother had begun reading it out of curiosity, only to have it snatched from her hands by her sister and hurled out of the window into the orange grove.

As we walked under the dark green leaves, where the scent of the fruit was sharp on the air, I wondered whether 'the devil's book' still lay out there, nibbled by mice and rotted by the leaves of many years. We passed a silent fountain and a building that had once been the coach-house and was now tottering into a last sleep. An old bridle hung on a nail outside and somehow there was still the smell and movement of horses round the creaking doors.

'There they are!' said Giulio.

They were sitting on a stone bench at the end of a long avenue of lemon trees. The sun was getting low and there was a hint of frost in the air. The smoke from the chimneys of the old house went up straight against the sky. Church bells began to chime in the blue distance.

'You should come and live out here,' said Giulio. 'We'd make a real Sicilian of you.'

'And how do I eat?'

'Oh, you could always eat—but it's true there are many hungry in the island. I think things will get better though—now they have found oil.'

'I'd like to come back one day,' I said, '. . . for good.'

TWENTY-THREE

THE weeks went by and we were borne along on the quiet stream of daily living. *Mother Goose* was now secured for the winter. She lay alongside the larger of the two galleons with a dozen fenders holding her cushioned against the rough wooden sides, and a gangplank across into the galleon's sally-port. It was convenient being there, for we had shore-lighting aboard, and our fresh-water tanks were topped up every week by old Gaspare. He had made his night-quarters in the galleon and acted as watchman for both of the boats. I would often hear him singing in the night watches, a scratched voice interrupted by eloquent silences when he took another swig from the bottle. 'Bedda Fontana' ('The Beautiful Fountain') was a favourite of his, and there was another, a love song with a refrain to it:

> Flower of the Fennel,
> When you walk, my eyes follow you. . . .

Our days followed a simple routine. About seven o'clock I would wake to hear Gaspare shuffling down the gangplank. Before he went home to Mondello he would bring me a copy of the *Giornale di Sicilia*. I liked to keep in touch with the events of a world that was a far remove from our present life. Not that the *Giornale* devoted much space to world news; Sicilian politics and Papal pronouncements usually made its headlines.

Unlike many of the fishermen Gaspare could read, slowly though, and with his finger following each word. Usually he had some dry, cackling comment on the news. He was deceived by little. One day the paper was full of the downfall and death of a Russian police chief.

'Better a live dog than a dead king,' he croaked.

It was no wonder that Mussolini had failed to give the Sicilians any sense of their 'noble and imperial mission' to restore the Grandeur of Rome. I remembered that, when I had first come to the island in 1943 and had landed at Port Augusta, the cottages had been blazoned with the Fascist slogan: 'Better a day like a lion than a hundred years like a sheep.' But rhetoric did not impress the Sicilians. Their needs were man's basic need on earth—food, a home, a woman, and children to take over when you were old.

Sometimes Gaspare had a piece of local gossip to tell me, and he would sit and drink a cup of coffee while I shaved. One day his news was that he and his cousin were trying to buy a fishing boat from a family in Sferracavallo. The boat had been laid up on the beach for over a year, but the family were still unable to conclude the deal, although they badly needed the money. It was the usual trouble you found all over Sicily. The way the law worked, there was no question of primogeniture, and so, when a man died, his property was divided among innumerable descendants. This particular boat was owned in varying shares by thirteen people; eleven of them were in Sferracavallo and they had said, 'Yes, sell it.' The twelfth was in Rome and the lawyers had just managed to get his written, and duly witnessed, permission to sell. The trouble was that the thirteenth, a cousin of some kind, was in the States and no one quite knew his address. Until his signature was forthcoming there could be no deal on the boat. Its value was about one hundred pounds.

'It is crazy,' Gaspare said, 'but then the law was made by lawyers. That is how they get rich.'

Sicily was like Ireland in the prevalence of priests and lawyers, and in the passion for litigation. In a poor country, with a peasant population, people will always go to law at the drop of a hat. It is like the weekly lottery, a chance perhaps to make some money, and it is also one way in which simple, unlettered people can express their personality by obstructing others. Every deal in Sicily was surrounded by lawyers, buzzing like bluebottles over the scrapings of old lire and the frayed edges of decaying estates.

There was nothing you could touch in the way of property without there being some legal tangle snarled around it. Walking with Giulio one day through the great orange grove outside their town house I listened in amazement as he explained how various alleys subdivided pieces of the property, this from his own section, that from his aunt's, that from his mother's, his grandmother's, and so on. At one point where there was a small triangle cut off by paths on each side, he told me how each of the dozen or so trees were earmarked for one or other member of the family.

'But that's nothing,' he said. 'When you get on some of the country estates, or on the peasants' small holdings, even the trees are divided. You'll find one man owning the south side of an olive tree and another the north side. The subdivision can even go down to individual branches. I've known law cases over who owned a particular fruitful branch.'

Gaspare had a friend, Giovanni, also a fisherman but of another generation—somewhere in his middle thirties. When the war came Giovanni had been conscripted and sent in the army to the desert. He had run away three times, once—as he proudly told me—getting as far back as Tripoli from Mersa Matruh.

'I nearly got a boat to Naples, too,' he said. 'What was the point of staying in that sand? I didn't want any of it.'

'What did they do to you when they caught you?' I asked.

'Oh, each time they put me in prison. But I didn't care. They still have to feed me. And no one shoots at you in prison.' He had once seen the Australians in action, and he had never forgotten it.

'Vast men like savages charging at us. Barbarians!'

He had been captured that time, but to his disappointment his group of prisoners had later been recaptured by the Germans. As far as Giovanni was concerned he had not been 'liberated', and he was disgusted at being returned to his unit and given another rifle. Finally he had been sent back to Sicily and, during the confusion of the Allied landings, had managed to make his third and last escape. He had gone up into the hills behind Cefalù, into the wild Madonie range near Pizzo Antenna. He had lived there nearly a year with a band of other deserters, black-market grain operators, and men who were on the run for many reasons.

'We were free in the mountains,' he said.

They stole cattle, intercepted grain convoys, and lived off the land. Most nights they were able to sleep in local cottages but sometimes they had to take to the caves. Then, one day, units of the Italian army police and field guardians (a branch of the carabinieri who looked after law and order in the country districts) came out to clean up the area. It was the only occasion in the war that Giovanni had ever killed anybody and he was not ashamed of it. He had no quarrel, as he put it, with the Australians or with the English in the desert. His quarrel was with the State that had taken him from his wife and home and sent him abroad as a soldier. As far as he was concerned, the police and the carabinieri represented the State—Italy and not Sicily—the power that had tried to alter and remould his life.

'They came up the valley looking for us,' he said, 'but we were on the sides of the hills. I would never have shot this policeman—but he came through the trees and saw me. I had a German automatic and I shot him in the belly. Then I finished him off through the head.'

The police had finally retreated, leaving three dead behind them and four of Giovanni's group wounded. A few months later the band broke up and Giovanni quietly slipped back to Palermo and rejoined his family. He was a good family man and he loved his wife and children. One Sunday he invited us to take the midday meal with them. We were conscious of the honour he paid us, for if a Sicilian workman asked you to his home it meant that you were truly accepted. We ate better than we would have done aboard the boat or in many a restaurant, and I knew that he had spent nearly a week's wages on the food. It was touching to see him holding up his youngest son aged three in those great hands that could have strangled an ox. He was a very gentle man.

In the mornings, after Gaspare had shuffled off with his usual wishes that we had slept well and that the day would be good for us, we tidied the boat and got breakfast ready. Now that the sails were off her and stored ashore, and all the running-rigging was down and made up in coils in the fo'c'sle, we lived in *Mother Goose* much as we would have done in a small flat. The sea was with us only in the slop and scend when a north-easter was blowing and a swell was making into the harbour. Even in the rainy days the cloud-base was never right down on the head, and there was never that sensation of being boxed up in a lead coffin. Always, somewhere or other, those blue patches of Dutchman's trousers would gleam through, so that we knew the sky was still there and would soon be back.

In the mornings, while Janet worked about the boat painting, sewing, splicing, or putting a whipping on some rope that we would need in the spring, I collected the notes for my jewellery book or clattered out the chapters on my old portable. Just off the Via Roma, in one of the narrow alleys that led down to the old market, I had found a working jeweller whose shop might have come out of the sixteenth century. Cellini's *Treatises* came alive and vivid in the cool workroom where the light spiralled in soft and diffuse off the side wall of an old church.

There were jewellers' pattern books in the shop dating from the eighteenth century, and old account books going back over a hundred years. They made an interesting footnote to the lives of Palermo's rich and noble, for a jeweller's knowledge was almost as secret as the confessional. Only he knew why, after the death of the principessa, her eldest son had had most of the family gems reset and had given only half of them to his wife. Sometimes a small note in the margin: 'Diamond brooch to be reset. Centre stone to be made into a ring for Sra. T. Other diamonds to be made into earrings and delivered to Sr. T. in separate box' revealed T.'s long-dead passion for an opera singer who had been visiting Palermo in the winter of 1910. I had passed the old man that morning; T. was related to Giulio and he was well over eighty now.

There were two apprentices working for the jeweller, and the air in the backroom was always bitter with the scent of metal shavings—gold and silver mostly, for he was a conservative who did not really approve of platinum and palladium. His one concession to the modern world was a dentist's drill which he used, instead of the old foot-operated wheel, for cutting cameos and intaglios. He was just finishing a fine cornelian signet with a dolphin carved on it. Watching the old jeweller at work with burin or graver, or with the dop stick in his hand setting some stones into a brooch, I would lose all sense of time, date, or even locality. The whole of the Mediterranean was in his dark shop, his skilled hands, and his quiet patience.

Two narrow alleys away, another world exploded. This was the old market-quarter and you could buy everything there from flying fish to fireworks. Yet even here the values were much the same as in the jeweller's workshop, for it was the individual human being that counted: the individual voice crying from a stall, or extolling a basket of almonds: 'How beautiful these almonds! The children weep to taste these almonds!' Shopping in Palermo was a vivid part of human life, where barter, cunning, and wit all combined to further the pleasures of eating and drinking.

Under the lemon-sun of winter the cobbled streets gleamed with running water where butchers, flower sellers, and fishmongers washed down outside their narrow-fronted shops and market stalls. The street traders did not fit into narrow distinctions; on one stall there was a mixture of children's toys, sugar animals, plaster statuettes of saints, razor blades, old American army boots, and cotton dresses. At the corner, where two alleys met, there was always a fat middle-aged man, with a face like a glass of red wine, who sold cooked octopus as well as singing birds in cages. The sea smell was heavy around the lower end of the market where most of the fishmongers had their stalls. Lean dogfish lay cheek by jowl with octopus and squid, dappled mullet, prawns, mackerel, the clawless Mediterranean lobsters, and strange scaly monsters with huge heads; like St. Peter's fish, the Angler. (He had been taken by trawl out of the deep night of the sea, where his phosphorescent lure acted as a bait for the unwary, and those deep jaws had closed with a snap on many of the inquisitive.) Layers of *bacalao* lay on marble slabs, with jets of water playing over the yellow sun-dried flesh. From this sea-world we made our way up another passage bright with fruit and vegetables. Here were piles of oranges, lemons, and mandarins; roots of fennel and fresh herbs from the mountains; figs, grapes, sugary raisins, and the fat-leaved artichokes which grew in the fields outside the city.

'Water, sweet water!' cried one man on whose back was strapped a brass contraption like an old geyser. The water was flavoured with anis and cost a penny a glass.

'Lemons! Lemons! Lemons with the most beautiful sugar!' cried another who was pushing a chemist's jar on pram-wheels through the throng. On a hot day a glass of his lemonade was as clean and astringent as a spring among rocks.

Dark doorways and gratings underfoot threw out warm smells of baking bread or roasting coffee. Cavern-like entrances, lit only by fly-specked bulbs, disclosed the vaulting shadows of wine-casks. Sometimes we would sit happily in one of these, the only customers. The padrone was a friend of Gaspare and his wine was good and strong at fourpence a glass. Where the door opened on the street I would watch the passers-by like puppets on their miniature stage. Always there was a ceaseless flutter in the air, for Sicilians talk with their hands far more than Italians. A hand ballet conveys as much as many words.

Two women stopped in front of the door.

'How is it?' One gestured.

The other raised both her hands, palms upward, and gazed at the sky with mournful resignation. ('We must take what the good Lord sends.')

A look of commiseration and two hands supporting an invisible weight in the belly was her neighbour's comment. ('Not pregnant again?')

A sad affirmative from a head that nodded slowly like a doll's.

Her friend opened her hands with the fingers spread wide in the universal gesture. ('How many already?')

The pregnant woman held up seven fingers, and then made graduated steps with her right hand to show their ages.

Her friend comforted her by putting the palms of her hands together and bowing her head. ('We can but pray.')

The conversation was over and they moved off into the crowd.

Alone or together, Janet and I spent many mornings in that market. Afterwards we would meet Giulio, or his brother and his wife, or some of their friends in one of the smarter cafés. Usually we had our midday meal aboard the boat. Even after the film work we had little money to spare—

about four pounds a week—but it was possible to live reasonably on that. The siesta habit was now as firmly ingrained with us as with the locals, and it seemed unthinkable not to rest for at least an hour after lunch. Most of the shops and businesses closed for two hours or so in the afternoon and reopened in the evening. As much work was done as in other countries, but the pattern of it was different. Many people worked until seven or eight in the evening and it was not until then that the city began to come to life. Cafés and bars stayed open until the small hours so long as there were customers. The last cinema shows began about ten in the evening, and entertainments sometimes went on until one or two. It was nothing to find cocktail parties beginning at eight, followed by dinner parties at ten.

Through Giulio and his relations we had met many of the baroque nobility. Some of their town houses were timeless with treasures, from Greek and Egyptian art to eighteenth-century niello-work on the finger-plates of the doors. We were strange fish to them—English, and living for preference in the barbarity of a boat, we were almost as remote as if we had just stepped green-faced and helmeted from a flying saucer. They were kind and unfailingly courteous to us, yet we always knew that what they said about us behind our backs must be even worse than what they said to our faces about their friends. Only one of Giulio's relatives, Prince B., still smarting from some Anglo-Saxon discourtesy of the past, was so frank as to ask me:

'What would be the English word for *'simpatico'*?'

'There isn't one,' I said. 'We have to use your word or fall back on the French.'

'You know why?'

'No.'

'It's because the English are not *simpatico!*'

Later, when he found out that our weekly treat was to go to the puppet shows, he relented. He even showed us his coin collection—Greek, Roman, Byzantine, and from every period of Sicilian history. The day before we left Palermo for the last time, he gave us a silver stater with the head of Athene on one side and winged Pegasus on the other. It had been minted by the Corinthian colony of Argos in the Gulf of Arta in the third century B.C. and had been ploughed up in some of B.'s land west of Palermo in 1946. The head of Athene was as crisp as if it had been cut only yesterday.

But it was Gaspare who had introduced us to the puppets, even if it was Prince B. who later took us to the carver who made them. It was

Gaspare who had said one mild, misty night, 'You have not seen the *opra d'i pupi?*' in a voice of amazement.

'We never had time before,' I said. 'Not in Catania, or anywhere else.'

'Catania!' He spat over the galleon's side. 'They know nothing about the *pupi* in Catania.'

That evening we went to the puppets with Gaspare. The theatre was a ground-floor room, just off the long main street that ran up from the dockyard. We stopped at one of the many bars for a drink first, and Gaspare was mellow as summer by the time we bought our tickets and settled down on the wooden benches. The audience was mainly men of Gaspare's age and young boys—the middle generations were missing, for the cinema had long since claimed them. Except for the self-conscious shows, or the lavish productions that toured the world, the art of the marionettes was slowly dying. In Palermo it lingered longest, for the carvers and gilders of the carts perpetuated the old stories of the Paladins. You could still buy the little paper-back books with their crudely told histories in some of the local bookshops.

We bought sunflower seeds from the proprietor's wife who ladled them out into paper spillikins for us from a basket on her desk. Then the old barrel-organ in the far corner started, and the overhead light went out. That night we were somewhere in the middle of the Orlando saga and Gaspare gave me a great jolt under the ribs when the hero came on.

'Very brave!' he explained.

Most of the dialogue passed us by, for it was deep dialect and the hidden operators made few concessions to the Italian language, while their voices were even huskier than Gaspare's. When Orlando met the first of the Moorish knights there was a sigh through the audience. Then he lowered his vizor and put his hand down to his sword, and—'*Durlindana!*'—everyone shouted, as the famous sword came rattling up into the air. Gaspare was deep down and far away in the story, his lined face working as the stamp-stamp of feet began. With every battle the puppet masters stamped their feet in a steady rhythm. After a time it became part of our blood and I still hear it in my head whenever I think of the puppets.

'They pleased you?' Gaspare asked when we came out into the cool night.

'Very much—very much—and so many thanks. We shall go often now.'

'You must go on Friday,' he said, 'don't forget—on Friday. They are doing the death of Orlando. It will make you weep to see that brave man betrayed—dying like a wolf on the mountain!'

168

After that we went every week until we could even follow the dialogue. But I remember the first time best of all. It was nearly midnight when we walked down to the docks. The street was faint with mist and the lights in the wine-shops shone on small groups, each isolated in their private worlds. The mist was quite heavy over the harbour, and there was a steamer booming away somewhere beyond the breakwater. The mist was damp on *Mother Goose*'s coach-roof and her iron sides were cold.

TWENTY-FOUR

I HAD caught jaundice, and there was nothing I could do about it but
lie in my bunk for two or three weeks. At first, when my temperature
shot up to 103, I had thought it was sand-fly fever; not that there was
much of that in Sicily, and malaria was almost stamped out these days.
But then the other symptoms had developed, and there was no doubt
about it.

'A beautiful colour,' said the doctor at the clinic when I took him
along a specimen. 'Very typical. You know what our technical definition
for this colour is? Old Marsala, that's what we call it.'

'I've drunk enough of it,' I said. 'Maybe that's why I've got the
jaundice.'

'No. No.' He had finished his various tests by now. 'Not that. You
have a beautiful case of Weil's jaundice—lucky you got it here in Palermo.
If you had gone down with it when you were away in some distant place
sailing your little boat it might have finished you off. Weil's jaundice, yes,
very interesting. It's rat-borne, you know.'

'There's not a rat aboard the boat,' I said indignantly. 'There isn't
room for one, to start with.'

'No, of course not. But somewhere or other, sometime you have eaten
food that has been contaminated. It is very easy, rat-droppings get among
flour and grain or other food. Well, you must go to bed aboard your boat.
You'll have to have injections—two a day intramuscular, and one
intravenous.'

'That's fine,' I said, 'but who's going to give them to me?'

'Your wife, of course. Who better? Naturally you have a syringe?'

As a matter of fact I had got one in the medicine chest, but the reason
he said 'naturally' was because almost everything was cured in Sicily
by injections. Almost every family medicine cupboard revealed a
hypodermic on the top shelf.

'I don't think she'd be much good at it,' I said. I had suddenly remembered that Janet had a horror of hypodermics, and the sight of one was enough to make her break into a sweat.

'Of course she will,' he said firmly. 'She is a practical lady. She must be, to sail about the world in a small boat.'

He pressed a bell on his desk and a minute later Janet was shown in by one of the nuns who worked in the clinic.

'Your husband has jaundice,' said the doctor. 'It is nothing to worry about but he must have injections every day. Two in the . . .' He tapped his backside. 'And one in the vein here,' he pointed to my forearm. 'Now I'll just show you how the syringe must be used.' I looked at Janet. She was a bit pale, and her hands were clenched. The doctor got a small box out from his desk, opened it and began to assemble the syringe.

'I'll just give him one now,' he said, 'and then you can give him the second one. Now—here is the phial for the intramuscular. We give him one of these on the left cheek and one on the right——' I was just undoing my belt when there was a sudden scurry, and Janet was no longer in the room.

'It's no good,' I said. 'She can't stand the sight of those things.'

'How curious! Well, we'll have to see whether we can make some other arrangement. You're not well enough to come up here every day.'

He gave me the injections, and a few minutes later I felt as if I had been kicked hard on the backside. I was hobbling about the room, trying to preserve my martyred sang-froid, when one of the nuns came in. She was smiling as if at a very good joke and she went across and whispered something to the doctor. He looked up at me.

'You were right,' he said. 'It would appear that the lady went out of here, felt faint and then fell down the stairs. . . . But don't worry. They are attending to her head now.'

'Her head?'

'She fell and cut her head.'

Janet had tumbled down a flight of stone stairs, cut her head open and landed at the feet of the head sister. The nuns were still whispering and giggling as we left.

'They think I'm pregnant,' said Janet. 'They can't believe it was the sight of that bloody syringe. Apparently, everyone in Sicily is weaned on them.'

They had shaved off a round patch of hair in the centre of her head and put a great bandage round it.

'Well, you must admit it's funny,' I said. 'We both arrived looking normal, and now I can hardly walk, and you look like a "soldier from the war returning".'

Giulio's brother Enrico and his attractive wife Bianca were waiting for us outside in their car. We were still laughing when we reached the boat.

'But seriously, it is a problem,' said Bianca. 'I think I'll have to come in every day and give you your shots.'

'Thanks,' I said, 'that's fine. I suppose you are used to it?'

'Of course. I am always giving them to the children and to the dogs—and to Enrico for his hay fever. There's nothing to it. As a little girl I used to practise on an orange. It's just about the same consistency as flesh and muscle.'

Janet went rapidly out of the cabin.

'For God's sake,' I said, 'she's off again! Don't talk about it, please.'

Enrico looked outside. 'She's all right,' he said, 'sitting up on the foredeck and breathing deeply.'

So every morning, for over two weeks, Bianca would drop in when she was doing her shopping and shoot me full of bull's liver and some other curative.

'It's a good thing you're English,' said Enrico with a laugh. 'I wouldn't like to have a Sicilian dropping his pants in front of my wife. Everyone would say I was *cornuto*!'

Bianca blushed. 'I'll put horns on you as big as antlers,' she said, 'if you go on like that.'

It is a bad thing to fall ill in a small boat. There is little enough room at the best of times, and with one bunk down all day *Mother Goose* took on the look of a floating sick-bay. In the evenings, though, friends would drop in and sit in a row across the cabin from me, drinking, smoking, and passing on the local gossip. I was allowed three glasses of wine a day, but, as the doctor had said, 'coffee on no account'. He had smiled. 'Ah yes. As long as the Italian business man continues to drink up to twelve cups of espresso a day, my little clinic for diseases of the liver will never be empty.'

Sometimes if Janet had gone ashore at night Gaspare would drop aboard to inquire courteously about my health. I would get him to sit down and take a glass. After a drink or two the stories would begin to come: stories about the palazzi in the old days when Gaspare's father had been coachman to one of the nobility; and tales about sailing ships and fishing expeditions. As a young man Gaspare had been a hand in one of the sailing schooners which used to work the Kerkenah banks off North

172

Africa. He liked to remember those days and talk about runs ashore in Tripoli and Alexandria, when he had money in his pocket and no wife to worry about.

'Mornings of blue,' he said, 'and the city very hot in midsummer. I remember coming back to the harbour at Alexandria through such a morning, having left my girl still asleep, and the Moors were unrolling their mats in the street to pray to their god.'

'It is a good city,' I said, 'I spent two years there once.'

'You know the Street of Women, then? The one that runs down to the docks.'

'Rue des Sœurs, yes.'

'There were many bars there. Many entertainments and many women. Once I even slept with a black woman. She was a heathen, but otherwise she was not different to other women.'

He liked to talk about the men he had known in those old ships, and about the mate of the schooner who had lost a hand and wore an iron hook at the end of his stump.

'He was a big man and wild as a wolf,' said Gaspare. 'One evening in Tripoli a Moor pulls a knife on him in a bar. He strikes the man down with his hook and opens his face as if he was gutting a fish. Then he picks up the Moor and throws him out into the street. *Santuzza*—how he was a man!'

'When I get up again,' I said, 'I want to hear some bagpipes played—you know the bagpipes of Sicily. I have a friend coming up from England who would like to hear them too. He is a man dedicated to old musical instruments.'

'The *meusa*?' he said thoughtfully. 'Yes, we can find a man who plays the *meusa*. There are not so many now as when I was a boy. One evening though I will bring my "worry-chaser" and play to you.'

A 'worry-chaser' is the Sicilian name for the jew's harp, an instrument still popular in the island. I had often heard its plangent buzzing in out-of-the-way places, for the jew's harp was a favourite among peasants and shepherds. If Theocritus or Virgil were to return to Sicily it would be the 'worry-chaser' and not the 'light reed pipe' that they would hear in the uplands on drowsy summer days. In all our months in Sicily I had only once heard a reed pipe, and that was in the spring when we had landed at Agrigento and walked inland to see the temples. The almond blossom was heavy on the trees near the temple of Hera, and it was there that we had come upon a youth 'lying at ease under the shade and practising country music on a light reed'.

One wintry evening when the harbour was misted with rain and a wind was blowing from the west we heard the scream of a car coming down under the bridge along the main road behind us. There was a crash, the tinkling sprinkle of broken glass, silence, and then noise and confusion on all sides. I had just about recovered from my jaundice, and I joined Gaspare, Janet, and the many others who were running to the scene of the accident. The car had piled up against a lamp post and the driver had already been hauled out by the time we got there, and laid by the roadside. He was not a very good sight and he was dead. In fact, as we learned later, he had been dead for several hours. He had been hit over the head and put in the car, which had then been sent roaring down the road. If the car had caught fire, as had been planned, there would have been no evidence that the driver's death was anything other than an accident.

'It was a mafia business,' said Giulio. 'There's been a lot of trouble recently between the old and the new mafia.'

'It was a matter relating to another matter,' said Gaspare tactfully.

I never asked the old man questions about the mafia. I was a stranger in his country, and whether Gaspare himself was a humble *mafiusu* or not was no concern of mine. More nonsense had been written about the mafia than anything else in Sicily—not that it could be defended in any way, but it was easy to see how it had grown up. It had really originated as a protection society for the native islanders against their successive waves of conquerors, and the organization seems to have crystallized during the Bourbon period. Behind the nominal law of the occupying power, the mafia had dispensed its own rough justice and carried out the old secret law, the *lex talionis*—an eye for an eye and a tooth for a tooth.

When Giulio said that the murder was due to a quarrel within the mafia, between the old and the new, he was referring to the split in the mafia ranks which had been growing worse in recent years. Traditionally the mafia, the old mafia that's to say, involved itself with property, cattle, the orange plantations, and all the other sections of a primitive economy. But now that Sicily was involved in a large industrial development plan the possibilities for bribery, extortion, and blackmail were acquiring more and more of a Wall Street complexion. Problems of capital, finance, oil, and dam-building had brought into being a new type of mafia chief. He was a kind of cross between Huey Long and Al Capone, and often he had a Sicilian-American background. Between the old and the new mafia a silent civil war was raging, and only isolated incidents—a killing or a kidnapping—betrayed the struggle for power that was taking place.

The old mafia operated in simple but efficient ways, and when I had worked for a week on the tunny fishery outside Sciacca I had heard one incident that was typical of its methods. Just after the war a North Italian had opened up another tunny fishery along the coast. There was no complaint about that, for there was much unemployment and there was room for another *tonnara* in that place. But shortly before the *mattanza* (the killing of the tunny in the net known as the 'chamber of death') was due to take place, the local mafia told the Italian owner how much his dues would be for operating a *tonnara* off that stretch of coast. Maybe the new owner believed Mussolini's pre-war boast that the mafia had been extinguished, at any rate he refused to pay. On the night before the *mattanza* was due to take place his nets were mysteriously destroyed, and he could bring no one to book—for it was the fish which had destroyed the nets! The technique was simple and effective; one of the *tonnara* men in Sciacca had told me how it was done. He had put it all in that problematical, roundabout way which appeals to the Sicilian.

'Supposing,' he said, 'that the signore, perhaps, had some quarrel with the owner of a tunny fishery up the coast. Now what might the signore do? Well, it is always possible that he might take a small rowing boat by night and in the boat he might take the carcase of a sheep. (I believe it might be better if this carcase was a little old and odorous, and that it should be divided into a number of pieces.) The signore might row out silently into the centre of the *camera della morte* and scatter into the water the pieces of sheep. Now—so they say—the smell of the blood would frighten the great tunny who are already in the net so that they become disturbed. But that is not all—the blood will soon bring in from the deep sea the vile sharks. These beasts will try to get at the odorous meat in the net and the sharks will alarm the tunny and the other fish. Before long—so I have heard—what with the sharks trying to get into the net, and the tunny trying to get out, the nets are broken into pieces.'

That was how the mafia operated, and you could take it or leave it. But while you were in Sicily you would do better to take it. In the case of that tunny fishery, the loss of the nets and the catch cost the new owner well over a thousand pounds. The year after, when it was delicately hinted to him that his fishery needed protection, he was a little wiser and paid his dues.

The fact remained that the mafia was not without its benefits to the ordinary householder. It was often more efficient than the police, and most of the big houses in Palermo paid their dues in one way or another. A friend of Giulio had his house burgled and lost some jewellery, of little value except sentimental. The police were called in and offered small hope for its recovery, so Giulio's friend approached 'other quarters'. After all, as he pointed out, he paid for protection. All of it was returned within a week, and there was nothing to pay: that was part of the service. Robberies of that type might often be carried out by mafia members, but it was not considered ethical to raid their 'subscribers', and the mafia had its methods of disciplining the free-lance burglar. The famous post-war bandit, Giuliano of Montelepre, had been doomed from the moment that he ran foul of the mafia, instead of co-operating with it. The government and the carabinieri had claimed the credit for Giuliano's death, but a quiet nod of the head at a smart Palermo party had once indicated to me the man who was rumoured to have really been responsible for his death.

The man whom Enrico, by a deft movement of his sleek head, pointed out to me looked perfectly at home in the splendours of that palace. The noble ceiling was ripe with rococo nudes, the footmen were in livery, and there was gold plate on the side tables. It was a long way from the mafia that Gaspare knew of, or the simple extortion along the tunny-fish route.

I remember that party because it was early January, there was snow on the hills behind the city, and the feel of ice in the streets of Palermo. They were drinking hot wine in the taverns down by the docks, and in the alleys of the market the trade had switched to cooked artichokes, steaming slivers of lamb and kid, and boiled octopus. Inside our host's house footmen were placing the open charcoal braziers in the vaulted rooms and long corridors. They were noble tripods of almost Pompeiian design, some of silver, supporting a shallow dish in which the charcoal quietly fumed. They gave little smell, and every now and again one of the footmen would quietly winnow them with a plaited straw fan. (The common-or-garden *braceri*, which we had met with in poorer homes, were usually placed under the family dining table, with a long baize cloth hanging down all round to keep in the heat. Here, at the one table, sat Mamma knitting, Father reading a newspaper, and children playing games. They kept their legs tucked in under the cloth and it was certainly a good way of keeping warm.)

Titles had officially been abolished when the new Italian Republic had been formed after the war, but that was one further reason why in Sicily they were more recognized than ever. If the common Italians would be democrats, then the noble Sicilians would be nobler than ever. We were surrounded by princes and princesses, mere counts and barones being, in the phrase, 'a lira a basket'.

'Have a drink,' said Giulio. (He knew well that all nordics were several drinks below par, and needed a stiff shot of alcohol before thawing to Sicilian temperatures.)

He handed me a glass and I was conscious, as usual, of my ungainly hands and feet when compared with Giulio and his friends. In England I was considered short, and my hands and feet normal, but here I always felt like a bull in a china shop. Giulio was my height, but his hands were half my size and, as for his feet, they would have done credit to a model-girl. (I had recently gone hunting for a pair of plain brown shoes, and had gone through three shops before I found one where they stocked the equivalent to an English 'eight'.)

The party had the same formalized ennui that accompanied all such meetings of the upper classes. All the women were grouped at one end of the main salon, most of them sitting round the wall in a half-circle. The men gathered mostly at the other end talking business, scandal, and sport. Little had changed here since the early nineteenth century, and Byron's comment was still apt: 'They go to the theatre to talk, and into company to hold their tongues. The women sit in a circle, and the men gather into groups, or they play at dreary *Faro* or "Lotto Reale", for small sums.' Almost the only difference was that, in modern Palermo, Bridge had superseded the old card games.

'What are you doing tomorrow?' said Giulio as we were leaving.

'We're working on the boat,' I said. 'We go up on the slip next week, you know. We're getting *Mother Goose* ready for the spring.'

'Still, you will not work all day. Why not come shooting? You do shoot, don't you?'

'A little,' I said. I had an old twelve-bore aboard the boat, but I had hardly used it in the past year. I was a bad shot anyway, and I did not want to let down the English reputation for marksmanship.

'I'd love to come,' I said, 'but I won't shoot, though. Where's it going to be?'

The party was meeting on B.'s estate at Bagheria, and Giulio arranged to drive us out with him.

'Shooting what?' asked Janet when I told her.

'I don't know. I forgot to ask.'

Giulio was down at the boat next morning. He was very much dressed *pour le sport* in heavy English tweeds and country shoes. The back of the car was full of guns, game bags, and bandoliers stuffed with cartridges.

We went out along the coast road and the day was fine with the sun getting a little more strength in it already. The sea looked calm beyond the fertile coast and we passed many of the carts coming into town loaded with fruit and vegetables for the market. Giulio drove well, handling the car like a swift-precision instrument. His gloved hands on the wheel were steady and sure, and he had wrist muscles and forearms that would not have disgraced an Olympic fencer. He had driven in the great *Giro di Sicilia*, and if I have given the impression that men like Giulio were not courageous then I have phrased things badly. They were just as brave as the English, but in very different ways. Whereas Giulio had had no interest in pursuing a war that he knew was already lost—and so had fired all his anti-aircraft ammunition away—he would have fought hard for anything that he believed in. At the other end of the social scale Giovanni, who had deserted three times from the army, was a fine, hard-working seaman who would have suffered torture and death in the interests of his own family. Byron was right again, when he wrote to John Murray: 'You would not understand it. . . . I know not how to make you comprehend a people, who are at once temperate and profligate, serious in their characters and buffoons in their amusements.'

We went through the dusty village of Ficarazzi at about eighty.

'This car goes like a rocket,' I said.

Giulio smiled. 'That's appropriate just here. You know what the name of this village means?'

I thought for a moment. '*Razzi*,' I said. 'Rockets?'

'Yes. And *Fica*?'

We both began to laugh, for it must be one of the strangest-named villages in the world, but unfortunately untranslatable.

The green land round the great houses at Bagheria came up in a gentle wave on our right. We passed the Villa Palagonia, its stone dwarfs and grotesques leering at us, and went on a mile or so until we came to B.'s house. B. was there, also in a smart English tweed, with a gun as big as himself under his arm.

'We'll have a drink first,' he said. 'The boys are getting ready in front of the house. Haven't you brought a gun, Ernle? Only Giulio and I, then. What a pity!'

After our drink we went down the crumbling old marble steps towards the orange groves. I had no idea what we were after—wolves, quail, or pigeons—and then a shrill noise began to sound through the trees as dozens of small boys started beating through the long green acres. The two huntsmen loaded and came to the ready.

'Boom!' B. let fly on my right. A shower of dark leaves and pulped oranges came whirling down. 'Boom! Boom!' Giulio fired a second later—both barrels, I think—into another dense cloud of green. (I still had seen nothing.) Then, with the third shot from B., a small ball of feathers like an untidy powder-puff came toppling from the sky. I had no time to see what it was—lark, linnet, thrush, canary, or nightingale—for the cannonade was all round me now. Diced leaves spun through the air, old riddled oranges came splodging down, and the air was thick with marmalade and cordite fumes. Occasionally, with a sinister buzzing like a horde of maddened gnats, a shower of pellets ricocheted off the trunks of the trees and came back around our ears.

Soon both beaters and marksmen joined up in a last thunderous fusillade. (I was glad to see that none of the boys had been winged.) Our own side of the party had also emerged unscathed. I think our total bag was about a dozen small songbirds, maybe a little more.

The crack of the solitary huntsman had often disturbed us in quiet coves and anchorages, but this was the first time I had ever seen a real, imperial *battue*. It was true that the birds would taste good but the expenditure of shot and oranges could never justify it. Neither could the sad silence which haunts most of the woods and groves of Sicily.

After the violence of the morning the afternoon was drowsy and golden. The great house came slowly to life as doors were opened into forgotten rooms, and long corridors echoed with our footsteps.

'The family come out here in the summer,' said B., 'but in the winter no one lives here. It was different in my father's day. Then they kept both houses going all the year round. The coaches went backwards and forwards every day between here and the city.'

We climbed a small hill behind the house where a forgotten English garden had run wild, and ornamental fountains had long ago filled with autumn leaves. From there we looked down towards the sea, and the fishing village of Porticello. There were small boats out in the bay and the sail of a schooner trembled on the horizon.

TWENTY-FIVE

'Y ou are leaving us?' Gaspare came down the gangway for his evening chat.

'In a week,' I said. 'We have to go back to Malta. And then to England.'

'It has been a good winter,' he said. 'But soon I am finished as a watchman for the film company. Then I go fishing again with my cousin.'

'I shall miss that,' I said. 'The fishing.'

'One day we will go out together. When you come back.'

'Yes, when I come back.'

Mother Goose was gleaming with new paint and varnish. Her sails were bent on and all the running-rigging was new. The shrouds shone, and the mast gleamed like a chestnut. The sky over the city was deeper and softer than it had been for some months, there was a lift in the air at mornings, and soon the flowers would be spreading over the capes and headlands.

'What shall we do this evening?' said Janet. 'I've had enough work for the day. All the food's aboard now, except for the fresh stuff. I've just checked through the list.'

'Let's have dinner out. And then go up and take a last look at Monreale.'

'That's a good idea,' she said. 'Bianca told me there's a festa on in Monreale tonight.'

We ate at a small restaurant at the eastern end of the town, near Puleo's boatyard and the fishmarket. The room jutted out on piles over the water, and from our table we could see the whole sweep of the bay. We had the pasta with sardines which they always did well there, and while we were eating it the mandolin player came in. There were only two other tables occupied, and he played the songs that were popular on Rome radio that winter. His voice was as sugary as the lyrics, but it was off-set by the astringent treble of the mandolin.

'Can we have the fisherman's love song?' I asked when he came round with the hat. It was one of Gaspare's favourites. ' "I wait on the jetty." '

'Ah, a Sicilian song!'

His voice was a good deal better than Gaspare's at any rate, and the words were clearer. The fisherman waits on the jetty to see his love passing. Nothing can ease the passion he feels for her, and everything in the world seems upside down unless she will listen to him: 'Water burns me and fire slakes my thirst!' Then he sees her and suddenly it is spring, the air is like honey from the mountains, and she is beautiful as a sweet orange. But his dream is broken, for she taunts him for being only a fisherman and smelling of fish. The song ends:

> I wait on the jetty.
> I am only a fisherman.
> Fate made me a man to catch fish from the sea.
> One day you will come fishing with me.

The sun was down beyond the city and the mountains, but the bay was luminous. It was stirred by a gentle breeze and the night-boats were going out, their sails catching the off-shore drift of wind.

We had a white wine with our chicken, and flowering broccoli to follow. Afterwards we had a slice of *cassata*—creamy and stuffed with fruit, chocolate, and pistachio nuts.

'Do you remember the cribs at Christmas in all the churches?' said Janet.

'Yes, and the bagpipes on Christmas Eve.'

Outside many of the shrines, and even inside the churches, the bag-pipers played on Christmas Eve. They waited along with the rest of the people until the stroke of midnight, when all the lights went up and the cribs were displayed.

'Talking of bagpipes,' she said, 'I remember that time you went off with Tony and Gaspare to find one.'

Tony, my musicologist friend, had arrived in Palermo having spent several months wandering through Calabria. He had heard the Calabrian pipes, and his diary was stuffed with notes about their construction and the tunes they played in southern Italy. Now, nothing would satisfy him but that we should at once set off with Gaspare, find a bagpiper, and get him to play for us.

Most of the *cornamusa* players were shepherds and countrymen, and they were difficult to find in Palermo except at special times like Christmas Eve. We had started looking in the bars along the water-front, and finally worked our way up to the Kalsa. That was the oldest and strangest part of the city: it had a North African feel about it, and the alleys were so narrow you could touch each wall as you walked down the centre. We spent nearly two hours there, going from one friend of Gaspare's to another, and from one bar and wine-shop to another. But still we found no pipes. By midnight I was indifferent to any music, and even Tony had lost some of his drive; only old Gaspare—determined not to let the stranger down—was eager to press on through the night. At long last, in one of the toughest parts of the town, near the Piazza Ballaro, we found our man.

By two in the morning we were at the far end of a dark wine-shop, the padrone nodding in his chair by the bar, our table littered with bottles and glasses, while Tony took notes and Gaspare translated. The bagpiper hunched himself over his inflated goatskin, the drone boomed round the walls, and Tony grew rapturous over 'grace notes' unperceived by me. I hardly remember getting back to the boat, but I do remember that Gaspare had a two-litre bottle which 'we must finish before the dawn', and that Tony had somewhere or other acquired a child's set of Sicilian bagpipes. They seemed to make almost as much noise as the real article.

'That was a night,' I said. 'Well, we'd better pay up and go.'

As we came out of the restaurant a carrozza came spanking by and the driver hailed us. We did not often take them, for their rates were high and there was often an argument over the fare at the other end. Still, tonight we were on a party, and it would be pleasant to clatter through the evening streets and stop wherever we wanted.

We went through the Quartiere San Pietro and I asked the driver to take us past the Church of the Martorana. Half of it was Spanish, and half Byzantine. It was cheerful and bright inside and I think it was my favourite church in Palermo. Part of the ceiling was a rich royal blue sprinkled with gold stars, and I was sorry to think I would probably not have another chance to see it. Then we went past San Cataldo, and that was rather like San Giovanni degli Eremiti, only all the mosaics had gone a long time ago. There was so much in Palermo, and even after six months there were still so many things we had never seen.

'We must go out to La Favorita once more,' I said.

'We could do that tomorrow.'

La Favorita was the house that had been loaned to Nelson when he had lived here as Admiral of the Mediterranean Fleet. It was on the road out to Mondello and it was a favourite place for the newly-marrieds to have their wedding photographs taken. Perhaps the image of Lady

Hamilton had become fixed in the popular mind as a kind of fruitful Venus? She had lived in La Favorita during those Palermo months, and you could still see her bedroom on the top floor. The thing that interested me most was the framed copy of the old Fleet signals which hung on the wall of her room. It showed that either she or Nelson had been a practical organizer, even down to the smallest details. From La Favorita it was impossible to see Palermo Bay, and so Emma Hamilton had not been able to tell whether the British Fleet was coming into harbour or not. But in those days there had been a naval signal station on the peak of Monte Pellegrino, and all she had had to do was watch the flag hoists made at the signal tower; consult the signal chart; and see whether those wisps of coloured bunting meant that the admiral was on his way. From the moment that the flag hoist was made, until Nelson came bowling down the dusty road, she would have had several hours in which to get herself and the house ready for his reception. Those Palermo months always presented a problem to Nelson biographers: they did not like the way he dallied adulterous (and a little corrupted in other ways) in the Kingdom of the Two Sicilies. Too few of them, perhaps, knew Palermo and the gentle ambiance of the south. It was a curious thought that those idle sunny months may have been the happiest in their hero's life. Of course Nelson was a fool about women, but so are most sailors.

We went through a sleepy square whose name I have forgotten. It had an ornate fountain in the centre with dolphins and naiads shining through the veils of water. Triton was blowing a mossy conch, and a group of small boys were playing round the fountain. One of them ran across and jumped up behind us, hanging on to the back axle while the driver tried to flick him off with his whip. We found a few small coins and dropped them over the back and heard his 'Grazie!' as he tumbled off to retrieve them.

We passed the Politeama (playing *Tosca* that night), and then the Teatro Massimo like a great balloon in the dusk, and began the long climb to Monreale.

'Look,' said Janet, 'it's started already.'

Rockets were starring the sky and there was the distant clamour of church bells. The driver gestured with his whip.

'Festa!'

It was one of those evenings when the Madonna was going on a visit. Saints, and Madonnas, and Christs as well, go visiting in Sicily. Their statues, dressed in their best clothes, are taken down and mounted on elaborate litters for the procession. Then they are taken through the streets and alleys and squares, calling at other churches on the way and renewing acquaintance with their saintly relatives and friends.

In the main piazza we paid off the driver and got a seat in a café just across from the cathedral. There were crowds up there that night, not only the locals, but others like ourselves up from Palermo, and many who had come in from the country. Although it was a religious festa there was plenty of drinking going on in the bars, and there was a light, happy feeling in the air. The giant Norman shoulders of the cathedral were glowing in a rain of stars and orange flares, and somewhere down the square a man was letting off *murtali*, the rockets that swoosh up and explode with a flash and a bang like an air raid.

The bells were thunderous in that close air. You could feel the weight and swing of them as they tumbled the heavy notes through the sky. Other churches round about were joining in; some with a rapid chime; others with sonorous tenor tones; and from far away there came a deep BOOM! regular as a blacksmith's stroke on a dark anvil.

'You can feel the winter's over,' said Janet.

'Yes. It's a real spring night. Shall we take a look at the cloisters?'

They were cool, and there was a strange peace in them. I wished that I could walk there for an hour, every day of my life.

We went back to the café and ordered a bottle of wine. Soon afterwards the whole square went up in a hiss of rockets and golden rain. Roman candles were pop-popping in the background and their liquid globes of colour painted the old walls green and gold and blue.

'Here She comes.'

There were many young acolytes in front, then came the priests, and then more boys with banners and crucifixes. The crowd grew denser and swirled like a river as the Madonna came into sight. Her golden hair and enamelled cheeks were brilliant over the dark bowed heads and the olive faces and hands. (It was strange that here, as in many other places, the Madonna was fair, whereas in England she was always brunette and Italian—proof maybe that it is the unfamiliar which compels respect.)

'In the summer,' said an old man sitting next to us, 'almost every night there is a festa in Monreale. In the morning everyone is too tired to work!'

Behind the swaying litter, borne on the shoulders of a dozen sweating workmen in their best dark suits, came many worshippers. Most of them were women, and many of them old with wrinkled walnut faces and dusty black clothes. When the Madonna passed, all of us in the café stood up. As we sat down again, the old man leaned across.

'You are not Catholic? But you stood up. . . .'

184

'Yes,' said Janet.

'One year,' he said, 'there were some other foreigners here, and they did not stand up. So I said to them: "If the Queen Elizabetta of England went past, you would stand up. Why then do you not stand for the Queen of Heaven?"'

It was early in the morning when we got back to the boat. Gaspare was drowsing over his oil-stove with a sack pulled across his shoulders. The harbour was quite still and we could see the lights of a ship coming in from the north.

'The festa was good?' asked Gaspare.

'Magnificent!' I said.

'What a sight!' said Janet. 'All those fireworks, and I can still hear those bells.'

'Oh yes,' I said, 'we have heard the chimes at midnight.'

ENVOI

... i nunc et vitae fugientis tempora vende
divitibus cenis. me si manet exitus idem,
hic precor inveniat consumptaque tempora poscat.
                                   Petronius Arbiter

Go now, and sell your life, your fleeting life, for feasts and
riches. But as for me, when the end comes, I pray it finds
me here, and in this place demands the reckoning of my
days.

THE wind came from the Levant and leaned against our stern. Cape Gallo dropped away on our port quarter, and Monte Pellegrino was only a blue cloud a little darker than the sky.

The sun was warm enough to sit easy at the tiller, wearing only a pair of shorts, with the wind like a purr on the nape of my neck. Above the sea-noises I could hear Captain Kidd rattling away in his cage and airing his new vocabulary.

'*Cornuto! Cornuto!* Pieces of eight! *Merde! Cornuto!*'

Janet was busy on the fo'c'sle, fixing a long boat-hook to the tack of the jib.

'Ready!' she called.

I stood by the sheets as she hoisted the sail, and a few minutes later the boat-hook swung out, pushing the jib on the opposite side to the mainsail. The wind was dead behind us now and we were crossing the Gulf of Castellammare, goose-winged into a new year. She was sliding along so easily, with her clean hull and her new paint giving nothing away to the slip of the sea.

'She's going well.'

'Nearly five knots,' said Janet.

We had our morning coffee in two of the mustard-yellow mugs we had bought at the pottery in Bagheria. We had bought lots of plates, cups and bowls; and near my feet in the cockpit a new *quartara* sweated and gleamed. We had filled it from the water-tanks that morning, and it would keep our drinking water cool and fresh all day. The Sicilian *quartara* was porous, and the water steadily evaporating through the clay kept it cool, even in the hottest weather.

With noon the wind began to freshen, and soon we were leaping along in a smother of spray, with the sea building and pushing under our stern. Further down in the Gulf fishing boats were scudding to and fro, and just to seaward of us a big wooden coaster was going by under sail and engine. As she went past, we saw she was deep-laden with timber and registered in Crotone. She was bound for Marsala most probably, where she would pick up a cargo of wine before making her way north again to the thirsty heel of Italy. The wine in Crotone was not much good, and it needed the strength and body of the Sicilian grape to make anything of it. For ourselves, we had two big demijohns lashed each side of the mast that we had bought from Gaspare's friend in the market of Palermo. We drank some of the white with our lunch, and it went well with the salad, mortadella, and melon.

Cape San Vito, the north-westernmost point of Sicily, came abeam and we gybed and altered course towards Trapani. We passed close to the lighthouse, and we could make out the figure of the keeper standing in a patch of green near the white tower. The sky over the island was very clear, but there were wisps of high cirrus coming up from the east.

'I hope this Levanter doesn't hold,' I said.

'If it does, we'll just have to wait in Trapani until it changes.'

It would be no use trying to beat our way down to Malta in the teeth of a strong Levanter.

'Or run across to Levanzo?'

'That's an idea,' said Janet. 'I'd like to see Levanzo again.'

There was a sigh and a splash just by the stern.

'Our friends,' I said.

Four or five dolphins had come up around us, and now they began to play, sometimes rolling just in front of our bows like small boys under a hose, and sometimes leaping clear of the sea, level with the cockpit. 'Our friends', Gaspare had called them.

'Once,' he had said, 'when I was young, I was sitting in a cove near Mondello and playing my "worry-chaser". Suddenly I felt that I was no longer alone. I looked up—and there were two dolphins lying right in the shallow water. Their heads were out of the water and their bellies were on the sand. They were listening to me. I could have gone out and touched them. But I was a little afraid.'

He half believed that the souls of dead fishermen were reincarnated into dolphins, especially men lost at sea: these, perhaps, were two of his companions who had been lost from the schooner on a dark night of storm off the fishing grounds near Cape Bon.

The dolphins stayed with us all afternoon as we ran down the coast. The shore was never more than a quarter of a mile away, and we could see how green the land was after the rains of winter. Over our port bow the peak of Erice drowsed in its soft cloud, and near the *tonnara* of Bonagia a boat came skimming out with the wind lifting its lateen sail, and two men at the oars. They had a pailful of the small jade-boned gar-fish in the boat and we bought some for supper in exchange for corned beef and cigarettes.

'Lire are no use,' they said. 'We live out at the *tonnara*, and only go into Trapani once a month.'

'What do you think of the weather?' I asked.

'Levanter for two, three days. Where are you going?'

'Tra——' I said. 'No. Levanzo.'

'Levanzo—that's only a little place. Better go to Trapani. Trapani is better for the lady—lights and music in the evenings.'

They dropped their sail and we watched them rowing laboriously back to the buildings on the shore, making heavy weather of it in the rising sea.

'Well, which shall it be?' I asked. 'Lights and music for the lady, or the Cala Dogana at Levanzo?'

She eased off the mainsheet as I pushed over the tiller, and we altered course for Levanzo.

In the late evening, with the sun going down behind the silver rock, we came to the island. We could see the *Unione* putting out to sea, and someone was waving from the track that ran inland towards the vineyards. As we lowered the sails Pasquale jumped aboard and held out his hand.

'Happy return!'

We went ashore with him and found his wife waiting on the beach. She handed something to Janet.

'Flowers of the island,' she said.

The lighthouse on Capo Grosso was beginning to spin and shine, and across the narrow straits the mountains of Sicily were catching the last light. The wind was drawing off the land and there were many boats going out to fish the western banks.